"4" cheese risotto
1/4 C Fortina
1/4 C Gorgongola
1/4 C. bel paese
parmesan
1/4 C whipping creme

D0597775

Riso

R i s o

❦

Undiscovered Rice Dishes
of Northern Italy

❦

by Gioietta Vitale

WITH LISA LAWLEY

❦

CROWN PUBLISHERS, INC.
NEW YORK

Copyright © 1992 by Gioietta Vitale
Illustrations copyright © 1992 by Jennifer Harper
All rights reserved. No part of this book may be reproduced or transmitted
in any form or by any means, electronic or mechanical,
including photocopying, recording, or by any information storage
and retrieval system, without permission in writing from the publisher.

Published by Crown Publishers, Inc.,
201 East 50th Street, New York, New York 10022.
Member of the Crown Publishing Group.
Random House, Inc. New York, Toronto,
London, Sydney, Auckland
CROWN is a trademark of Crown Publishers, Inc.
Manufactured in the United States of America
Designed by Ken Sansone

LIBRARY OF CONGRESS CATALOGING-IN-PUBLICATION DATA
Vitale, Gioietta.
Riso: undiscovered rice dishes of Northern Italy /
Gioietta Vitale with Lisa Lawley.—1st ed.
p.   cm.
Includes index.
1. Cookery (Rice)   2. Cookery, Italian—Northern style.   I. Lawley, Lisa
TX809.R5V58   1992   91–43008
641.6'318—DC20   CIP

ISBN 0-517-58856-0
10 9 8 7 6 5 4 3 2 1
FIRST EDITION

To
my mother and father,
who taught me how to enjoy
the beauty of the simplest gifts
of nature

Contents

Introduction

*T*his book is dedicated entirely to rice—specifically Northern Italian rice and its various uses. Having grown up in Milan and lived in New York for many years, I'm delighted to see the flurry of interest here in risotti, the classic rice dishes of my home region. However, I would like to emphasize that the Northern Italian appreciation of rice goes much further than risotti; like pasta in the south, the grain is an important ingredient in many of our favorite dishes. In fact, you might say it is our pasta. It is my pleasure to share with you here a number of dishes using rice—soups, salads, primi piatti, and desserts (though not too many of these last)—that I have enjoyed serving over the years.

The earliest written reference to rice cultivation in Italy dates from the fifteenth century, but rice probably was introduced to Italy in the tenth century, most likely as a result of the Saracen invasion. These marauding Arabs brought to Sicily and *the mainland some of their favorite foods, including citrus fruits, sugarcane, and almonds. The history of rice—the edible seeds of an annual grass—is considerably more ancient than its appearance in Italian cuisine, possibly even older than wheat. The first confirmed site of rice cultivation was at what is now Non Nok Tha, Thailand, in about 3500 B.C. From there, during the next two millennia, rice cultivation slowly spread to China and India, where it became an important staple food and was eventually passed to the Arabs in the course of trade. According to the International Rice Research Institute in the Philippines, approximately 30,000 varieties of rice exist—although by another count, as many as 30,000 varieties may once have been cultivated in India alone. Today rice is grown in almost every part of the world, and total production is estimated at 400 to 420 million tons per year.*

In Italy, rice is cultivated in water—planted in April and ready to harvest by September. The rice grown along the Po Valley in Piedmont, Lombardy, Emilia, and Veneto has special properties that have lent it to a wide variety of uses. This rice has the ability to absorb large amounts of liquid while retaining the shape of the grain and remaining firm. And the grains of Italian rice, when cooked, release just the right amount of amylopectin (a type of starch) to enable the grains to cling nicely without becoming glutinous or sticky.

Arborio rice is the Italian rice most widely available in the United States, where it can be found in many supermarkets as well as in gourmet food shops and

Italian grocery stores. Arborio makes a fine risotto with firm, separate grains and works as well in salads and other recipes. I've used Arborio rice in all the recipes in this book, but the table on page 12 lists the other Italian types and their properties. You may substitute them for the Arborio where appropriate—but you are unlikely to run into the other varieties very often in this country. Most Arborio rice sold in the United States is packaged in cloth or cellophane bags and has been thoroughly cleaned. (If you happen to buy your rice in bulk, you will need to pick over it carefully and wash it in cool water a couple of times before cooking.) In the summertime, or if you live in a hot, humid part of the country, it's best to buy only as much rice as you can use in a week. Store the rice in a tightly sealed container to prevent the oils in the grains from breaking down and turning rancid when exposed to the air. This way your rice will always have the freshest possible taste.

The cooking times given in the recipes and the table on page 12 are approximate. The altitude, humidity, and individual properties of your stove may affect the cooking time, so it is very important that you taste the rice near the end of the suggested cooking time. If the rice is al dente—firm to the bite, but with no chalkiness at the center—remove the rice from the heat and serve immediately. Otherwise, the rice will continue cooking even after it has been removed from the stove. (Some recipes that require further preparation call for the cooked rice to be rinsed immediately in cool running water; this is to arrest the cooking process and keep the rice from becoming mushy.)

Aside from this caution, however, you will find the recipes in this book simple and quick to prepare, a boon whether you are cooking for guests or for your family. Some of the dishes are robust and warming while others are ultralight—the perfect showcase for perfect summer fruits and vegetables. Best of all, rice is an extremely healthful food. Its complex carbohydrates make it easy to digest (remember when plain rice was a commonly prescribed treatment for an upset stomach?) and rich in B vitamins, iron, and calcium. In addition, most of the recipes in this book contain only small amounts of butter, cream, or meat, and quite a few are entirely

Italian Rice Varieties

TYPE OF RICE	TRADE NAME	SHAPE	USE	COOKING TIME
Ordinario (common)	*Balilla*	*fat and round*	*cakes soups*	*10 minutes*
Semirefined (semifino)	*Maratello*	*medium long*	*soups risotto*	*15 minutes*
Fine (fino)	*R.B. Razza 77 Vialone*	*long*	*risotto*	*16 minutes*
Super-refined (superfino)	*Arborio Carnaroli*	*long and fat*	*risotto*	*18 minutes*

vegetarian. Once you become acquainted with the Northern Italian way with rice, I am sure you will agree that this venerable grain has at least as much to offer the busy American cook as pasta.

Some Notes on Ingredients

HERBS ✧ *Italian food is a cuisine of simple, clear tastes. Often the flavor of a dish is built around a single herb or, at most, two complementary herbs. For this reason, it is best to use only fresh herbs, which give the strongest, truest flavor, when preparing the dishes in this book.*

BASIL is probably the herb I use most often. This annual plant, which grows in the world's temperate and subtropical regions, is widely cultivated for kitchen purposes and is believed to be an excellent soothing element for upset stomach symptoms as well as for headache relief. Basil may be seeded in greenhouses in March or April, or outside if it is brought inside the house at night. By May, it is safe to transplant the young plants outdoors, where they will need frequent watering. The plants will send up spikes of white or pinkish flowers. When picking basil leaves for cooking, pinch off the tops of the plants in a cluster (never pinch off single leaves). Pinching the tops encourages the basil plant to develop in a bushy, full shape and to send out new shoots that will keep you in basil all summer long. Since basil is an annual, it won't last forever, but you can extend the life of your plants by potting and bringing them indoors before the first frost in October or November. The pots should be placed in a sunny window. Luckily, when your homegrown basil runs out, these days you can usually buy fresh basil in the supermarket year-round. Fresh basil has a strong, pungent aroma, and your food won't need any other seasoning. The leaves have an oval shape and a deep green (or sometimes purple) color that makes a beautiful decoration for a platter.

PARSLEY is a biennial plant of the carrot and parsnip family that originated in Europe. It is widely used as both a garnish and a flavoring for food. It has deep green, aromatic leaves and comes in two varieties: curly and flat-leaf. Some people think the flat-leaf variety is more aromatic than the curly parsley, which perhaps looks more attractive on a plate. Parsley is very easy to cultivate and spreads profusely in the garden with little encouragement.

OREGANO, a member of the mint family, is a perennial that grows wild in the Mediterranean region and is cultivated all over the world. Oregano has a very strong scent, thick, somewhat fleshy leaves, and pretty lavender flowers. It is a favorite seasoning for Italian food. Although fresh oregano is preferable, it can also be hard to find. You can always use the dried herb, but use only a quarter of the amount you would when using fresh.

SAGE is also a member of the mint family. This perennial has soft, aromatic gray-green leaves and delicate purple-blue flowers, which usually blossom in June or July. Fresh sage is always preferable to dried, but, again, if you can only find dried sage, use only a quarter of the amount you would when using fresh.

SAFFRON ✧ *Saffron is a very strong seasoning that has been used in the culinary arts for centuries. Saffron is the dried stigma of the blossoms of* Crocus sativus, *a plant native to Asia Minor and grown widely in Europe. Each of the tiny stigmas must be gathered by hand, and it takes thousands to make an ounce—which explains why saffron is rather costly. However, a little pinch will permeate a dish with its lovely strong scent and give it a beautiful orange color. I use saffron in my Risotto alla Milanese and in a couple of other dishes.*

GARLIC ✧ *In the United States, garlic sometimes seems synonymous with Italian cooking. I am afraid this is not exactly true. We do use garlic, but, particularly in the north, we do not abuse it. You will notice that in this book, garlic is always discarded from a dish after only a very short cooking period.*

Please be very careful when using garlic. The garlic you use should always be very fresh. When you buy garlic, look for a large, fat, turgid white head; this garlic is sweet and will last longer in your pantry. When you peel garlic, the cloves should be pure white in color and never wrinkled or withered. Discard any cloves that are not immaculately fresh.

TRUFFLES ✧ *The truffle's reputation as a choice table delicacy is well established owing to the relative rarity of this fungus and the hubbub that surrounds its* *harvest each fall. With the help of trained pigs and dogs, the truffle is dug up from the roots of the trees it favors for its symbiotic subterranean life. Truffles have a round, tuberous shape and an exterior surface that can be either smooth or wrinkled. The magnatum truffle—the white truffle found near Alba, Italy—is considered to have the most delicate taste. Other varieties include the melanosporum, or black, truffle, harvested near Spoleto, Italy, and Perigord, France; and the rarer excavatum (yellow) and brumale (violet) truffles. All these varieties grow in symbiosis with the root systems of certain hardwoods, including poplar, oak, willow, and hazelnut trees.*

Truffles are eaten raw, which is the best way to appreciate their strong, earthy, and aromatic flavor. They may be grated over risotti, eggs, rice, pasta, carpaccio, or other dishes.

The best way to store truffles at home is to place them in a sealed jar filled with rice. The rice will absorb the truffles' aroma and will make a wonderful risotto.

PORCINI MUSHROOMS ✥ *Fresh porcini mushrooms are still difficult to find in the United States, except in New York and a few other cities; even in these communities, it is still often a matter of luck whether you are in the right place at the right time. If you do happen to find fresh porcini, do not hesitate to buy them, since their taste is like nothing else.*

When using fresh porcini, never peel the mushrooms—and do not wash them, either. Wipe away any clinging dirt or grit using a damp paper towel. Do not remove the spongy underside of the porcini caps unless it is soggy and spoiled.

The recipes in this book call for dried porcini, but you can easily substitute fresh. Simply slice the cleaned mushrooms and sauté them briskly for a minute or two in olive oil or butter until they begin to release their liquid. Reduce the heat and simmer fifteen to twenty minutes until most of the liquid has evaporated. Add the mushrooms to the dish you are preparing as you would reconstituted dried porcini.

Dried porcini are found in Italian groceries and in many supermarkets. Try to purchase dried porcini in packets that enable you to examine their color and condition. Look for large, light-colored mushroom pieces; darkened, crumbled mushrooms are usually past their prime. One ounce of dried mushrooms is the approximate equivalent of three-quarters pound fresh.

Dried mushrooms should be soaked in lukewarm water for at least twenty minutes before using them in a recipe. After the mushrooms have soaked and softened, gently fish them out of the water, being careful not to disturb the sediment that has settled at the bottom of the dish. Rinse the mushrooms several times under cool running water to remove any remaining dirt. As with fresh spinach, you don't want to spoil your risotto by adding sand along with the porcini!

The porcini soaking water can be used to add extra flavor to a risotto. Simply filter out any particles by pouring the liquid through a wire strainer lined with a paper towel. Use the flavored liquid in place of part of the broth.

OLIVES AND OLIVE OIL ✧ *Olives are the small fruits of an evergreen tree called* Olea europa, *which originated in the Mediterranean area. When ripe, these fruits are processed and eaten alone or as part of many kinds of dishes. Americans are very familiar with Spanish, Greek, and Italian olives, but olives are also produced in many areas of the Middle East.*

I am very fond of olive trees. They are all beautiful and majestic, and many are quite ancient, perhaps a thousand or more years old. As a child, my summers were spent in Liguria along the Italian Riviera, where my family owns an olive grove covering part of a collina, *or hill. The contorted, dark trunks of the olive trees contrasted with the fragility of their peculiarly shaped rounded leaves, which are green on top and gray on the bottom. When the wind blows from the Mediterranean Sea, the* collina *show green, and if it blows from the mountains, the* collina *flash silver. It is an unforgettable sight.*

In Italy most of the olive crop is used for making oil. Harvest time varies by year and location; in Liguria, it may come as late as January, and in the south of Italy it can be as early as October. Nets are placed under the olive trees, which are then shaken vigorously. The ripe olives fall into the nets and are taken to the frantoio *(press) to be ground and pressed. Olive oil is simply the pure juice of ripe olives— skins, pits, and all—extracted from these pressed olives. No chemicals or heat should be used in the pressing, although you may encounter an unpalatable brand with a bitter taste indicating that these shortcuts were used to increase the yield.*

To avoid this, look for one of four labels when buying Italian olive oil. The best-quality olive oil is called extra-virgin *and contains less than 1 percent acidity. Second best is* superfine virgin, *with 1 to 2 percent acidity. Third and fourth are* fine virgin, *which contains between 2 and 3 percent acidity, and* virgin, *which may go up to 4 percent. "Pure" olive oil is a still lesser grade.*

I recommend that you use extra-virgin whenever possible, especially in salads, although it costs a good deal more. For frying or for making risotti, superfine or fine virgin oil works well.

PARMIGIANO REGGIANO CHEESE ✢ *In the United States the word* Parmesan *is used for all kinds of cheeses that have nothing to do with the real thing,* Parmigiano Reggiano, *which is produced under carefully controlled conditions by only a few specialized cheese makers in the areas near Parma, Reggio, Modena, Mantua, and Bologna. Many years ago it was impossible to buy Parmigiano in the United States, and my father, who owned a farm near Parma, would give us half a wheel (and sometimes even the entire wheel) when it came time to return to New York. Though it was difficult to handle this monstrosity, the U.S. Customs agents were always very nice to us, and we somehow always managed to get it home with the children and all our luggage. Once home, we had to divide the cheese into more manageable pieces and coat the cut surfaces with a special wax, which we applied with brushes.*

These days, enjoying Parmigiano Reggiano in the United States is much easier. You should always buy your Parmigiano at an Italian grocery or gourmet shop of good reputation. The cheese you are looking for comes in a big yellow wheel with the words Parmigiano Reggiano *stamped in black dots on the rind. Make a point of getting to know the owner of the grocery where you buy your Parmigiano. Once he knows you are a good, appreciative customer, he will be proud to advise you which cheese is the best and a good buy.*

Never, never buy grated Parmigiano, even if the storekeeper swears on his wife's head that he just finished grating it the instant you walked into his shop. In order to have freshly grated Parmigiano whenever you need it, buy a larger quantity than you can use right away. When you get home, cut the cheese into two pieces for storage in the refrigerator, one in the amount you plan to use right away. Seal the pieces of cheese carefully with plastic wrap. Make sure the cheese is carefully rewrapped each time you remove it from the refrigerator for grating. Check your cheese periodically. If it has dried out, wrap a damp piece of cheesecloth around it and refrigerate overnight. By morning, its texture should be restored and you can remove the cheesecloth and rewrap the cheese in plastic. Be careful not to store the cheese in the coldest part of your refrigerator.

For familiarity, the word Parmesan *is used in the recipes in this book, but you should remember that it always refers to the real Parmesan—Parmigiano Reggiano.*

Some Notes on Kitchen Tools

The recipes in this book require very little in the way of specialized equipment. One very important item, however, is a colander, which you will be using quite a lot. Your colander should be very sturdy and have a supporting base (usually four little legs) and handles so that you can easily drain your rice. A good colander is made of stainless steel or aluminum, to avoid rust.

Another "must" is a grater for your Parmesan cheese (which is vital to the success of your risotti), and also for the occasional truffle. You may choose either a flat or a four-sided grater, whichever you find easiest to handle. Again, this tool should be made of stainless steel.

For mincing vegetables for your risotti and other recipes, you may find the half-moon cutting tool called a mezzaluna *useful.*

A couple of two-quart ring molds will come in handy when serving your insalate di riso. *They make an impressive presentation out of a simple dish.*

Finally, to stir risotti, I am very fond of my long wooden spoon. The wooden spoon is very sturdy, helpful with the large amount of stirring required for risotto; it also enables the cook to stand back from the stove a bit, so that the odor of sautéed onion does not penetrate hair and clothes. (Remember, risotti must be prepared just before serving, so you will not have a chance to freshen up and change clothes before serving your guests.)

Minestre

❧

SOUPS

Meat Broth

Chicken Broth

Vegetable Broth

Fish Broth

Rice Soup with Parsley

Rice Soup with Leeks

Rice Soup with Asparagus Tips

Spinach-Rice Soup

Soup with Rice and Peas

Tomato-Rice Soup

Milk-Rice Soup

Vegetable-Rice Soup

Lemon-Rice Soup

Rice Soup with Chicken Livers

Minestrone alla Milanese

*T*he foundation of a great soup is great broth. And the best broth, we all know, is homemade broth. Though it's not difficult to make, homemade broth does require time and patience—two commodities quite rare these days.

However, if you do prepare your own broth (and I hope you will), your efforts will be rewarded. The following two simple guidelines will make you wonder why you ever considered making broth difficult or not worthwhile:

1 ☙ Keep in mind that broth is best when light in taste. To achieve this lightness, use meat free of excess fat—and above all, use good-quality ingredients. This is very important, since you will be using your homemade broth for tasty risotti, soups, and other dishes. You do not want to spoil your cooking with broth that is anything less than first-rate. By educating your palate to simple, genuine taste by using prime meat products, fresh herbs, and ripe produce, you will come to understand that quality is far more important than quantity. And if you understand this, then you are already a good cook.

2 ☙ As long as you are taking the time to prepare homemade broth, make a large quantity. You can freeze whatever you don't need immediately in convenient portions for later use.

If you find that you have no homemade broth on hand, my preferred storebought alternative is Knorr's bouillon cubes.

Brodo di Carne

M E A T   B R O T H

This recipe features a combination of meats that I like, but feel free to vary the proportions to suit your taste.

> 2 *pounds chicken parts, excess fat*
>   *removed*
> 2 *pounds boneless veal, fat removed*
> 2 *pounds boneless beef, fat removed*
> 1 *pound beef bones*
> 4 *teaspoons salt*
> 2 *medium onions, peeled*
> 2 *celery stalks*
> 2 *large carrots, peeled*
> 1 *small potato, cut into quarters*

↬ Rinse the chicken, veal, beef, and bones under cold running water.

↬ Place 4 quarts water and the salt in a large stockpot. Bring water to a boil over high heat, then add the chicken, veal, beef, bones, salt, and vegetables and return to a full boil.

↬ After 5 minutes, reduce the heat to low and allow the broth to simmer very slowly, with only an occasional bubble breaking the surface, about 2½ hours. Skim foam from the top from time to time.

↬ Remove the meat and vegetables from the pot. Strain the broth through a fine linen towel or double thickness of cheesecloth, then refrigerate. When the broth is chilled, skim any solidified fat from the surface.

↬ Use fresh broth as needed. Store leftover broth in plastic containers in the refrigerator or freezer. Broth will keep 4 to 5 days in the refrigerator and up to 1 month in the freezer.

M A K E S   3   T O   4   Q U A R T S
↬

Brodo di Pollo

CHICKEN BROTH

1 whole chicken (about 3 pounds)

1 tablespoon salt

2 medium onions, peeled

2 celery stalks

1 medium potato, cut into quarters

↬ Rinse the chicken in cold water and cut off any visible fat.

↬ Place 3 quarts water and the salt in a stockpot large enough to hold all ingredients comfortably. Bring the water to a boil over high heat. Add the chicken and vegetables and cook at a full boil for 5 minutes. Reduce the heat to low and simmer the broth very slowly for about 2 hours, skimming the foam from time to time.

↬ After 2 hours, remove the chicken from the broth with a slotted spoon. (The chicken may well be in pieces at this point.) Strain the broth through a colander lined with 2 layers of cheesecloth or a kitchen towel and refrigerate the strained broth. When the broth is chilled, skim off any fat that has accumulated on the surface. Store broth in containers in the refrigerator or freezer. Broth will keep 4 to 5 days in the refrigerator and up to 1 month in the freezer.

NOTE: I usually make a chicken salad with the broth meat. I discard all the bones and cut the chicken into bite-size pieces. Then I add some olive oil, some minced parsley, a couple of olives, and salt and pepper to taste.

MAKES 3 QUARTS

↬

Brodo di Verdura

VEGETABLE BROTH

This kind of stock is very handy for making vegetable-based risotti—or any other dishes you want to give a light, delicate flavor.

3 celery stalks

3 medium carrots

3 leeks, white parts only

2 medium tomatoes

3 bunches fresh spinach

1 bunch fresh parsley

2 medium onions

4 fresh basil leaves

½ tablespoon salt

Wash the vegetables, paying special attention to the leeks and spinach. Peel and trim the vegetables as necessary, making certain to remove the tough stems from the spinach, and cut the celery, carrots, and leeks into 3-inch lengths.

Place the vegetables in a large stockpot with the basil and the salt. Add 4 quarts water and bring to a boil. Reduce the heat and simmer at least 1½ hours, skimming any foam from the top as necessary.

Remove the stock from the heat and strain through a wire strainer lined with cheesecloth. Allow the stock to cool. You can use the stock immediately, or refrigerate or freeze for later use. The stock will keep 4 or 5 days in the refrigerator and up to 1 month if frozen.

MAKES 1½ TO 2 QUARTS

Brodo di Pesce

FISH BROTH

2 pounds fish bones, heads,
    and/or trimmings from any
    delicate white fish
1 bottle dry white wine
½ cup fresh lemon juice
1 medium onion, peeled
2 bay leaves
1 bunch fresh parsley
3 medium carrots, cut into pieces
1 teaspoon salt

✤ Place all the ingredients in a large stockpot with 2 quarts cold water. Cover and simmer for about 1 hour. Strain broth through a colander lined with 2 layers of cheesecloth or a kitchen towel. Refrigerate the strained broth and store in containers in refrigerator or freezer. Broth will keep 4 to 5 days in the refrigerator and up to 1 month in the freezer.

MAKES ABOUT 2 QUARTS

✤

Minestrina di Riso e Prezzemolo

RICE SOUP WITH PARSLEY

2½ quarts Meat, Chicken, or Vegetable
    Broth (pages 27 to 29), or 2½
    quarts water plus 2 bouillon
    cubes and ½ tablespoon unsalted
    butter
1 cup Arborio rice
5 tablespoons finely chopped parsley
Salt to taste
Freshly grated Parmesan cheese

✤ Place the broth (or water, bouillon cubes, and butter) in a large stockpot and bring to a boil over high heat. Add the rice to the broth, reduce the heat to medium, and simmer, checking for doneness after about 16 minutes. Rice should be al dente, or firm to the bite; do not overcook.

✤ When the rice is done, stir in the parsley and salt to taste. Serve immediately, with Parmesan cheese at the table.

SERVES 4

✤

Minestrina di Riso e Porri

RICE SOUP WITH LEEKS

1 medium leek

1½ quarts Meat, Chicken, or Vegetable Broth (pages 27 to 29), or 1½ quarts water plus 2 bouillon cubes and 1 tablespoon unsalted butter

½ cup Arborio rice

Salt to taste

Freshly grated Parmesan cheese

 Thoroughly wash and trim the leek, checking carefully to see that all sand has been removed, then cut it into bite-size chunks.

 Place the broth (or water, bouillon cubes, and butter) in a large stockpot and bring to a boil over high heat. Add the rice and leek, reduce the heat to medium, and simmer, checking the rice for doneness after about 16 minutes. Rice should be al dente, or firm to the bite; do not overcook.

 Taste, and add salt if needed. Serve immediately, with Parmesan cheese at the table.

SERVES 4

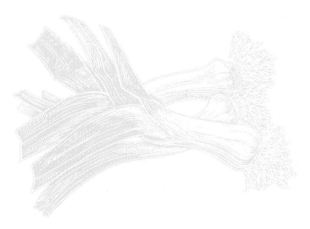

31

Minestrina di Riso con Punte d'Asparago

RICE SOUP WITH ASPARAGUS TIPS

2½ quarts Meat, Chicken, or Vegetable
Broth (pages 27 to 29), or 2½
quarts water plus 2 bouillon
cubes and 1 tablespoon unsalted
butter

1½ cups Arborio rice

8 asparagus tips, trimmed

Salt to taste

⤙ Place the broth (or the water, bouillon cube, and butter) in a large stockpot and bring to a boil over high heat. Add the rice and asparagus tips, reduce the heat to medium, and simmer, checking the rice for doneness after about 16 minutes. Rice should be al dente, or firm to the bite; do not overcook.

⤙ Taste, and season with salt, if needed. Serve immediately.

SERVES 4
⤙

Minestrina di Riso e Spinaci

SPINACH-RICE SOUP

*1½ pounds fresh spinach, or 1 10-
     ounce package frozen spinach,
     thawed*

*1 quart Meat, Chicken, or Vegetable
     Broth (pages 27 to 29), or 1
     quart water plus 2 bouillon cubes
     and 1 tablespoon unsalted butter*

1 cup Arborio rice

Salt to taste

Freshly grated Parmesan cheese

✢ Carefully wash the fresh spinach in cool water, repeating several times. Dry each leaf individually with a clean kitchen towel to make sure all dirt and sand has been rinsed away. This is very important, since even a grain or two of sand will ruin the soup.

✢ Place the broth (or the water, bouillon cubes, and butter) in a large stockpot and bring to a boil over high heat. Add the fresh or frozen spinach and the rice, reduce the heat to medium, and simmer, checking the rice for doneness after about 16 minutes. Rice should be al dente, or firm to the bite; do not overcook.

✢ Taste, and add salt if needed. Serve immediately, with Parmesan cheese at the table.

SERVES 4

✢

Minestra di Riso e Piselli

SOUP WITH RICE AND PEAS

5 cups Meat, Chicken, or Vegetable
   Broth (pages 27 to 29), or 5 cups
   of water plus 2 bouillon cubes
   and 1 tablespoon unsalted butter
½ cup Arborio rice
2 cups shelled fresh peas, or 1 10-
   ounce package frozen early peas,
   thawed
1 tablespoon unsalted butter
1 tablespoon all-purpose flour
Salt to taste
Freshly ground black pepper to taste

✤ Place 4 cups of the broth (or water, bouillon cubes, and butter) in a large stockpot and bring to a boil over high heat. Add the rice and peas, reduce the heat to medium, and simmer.

✤ Meanwhile, place the remaining 1 cup broth in a small saucepan over medium heat. In a small skillet over medium heat melt the butter. Add the flour and stir briskly with a wooden spoon until the roux turns light brown. Add the 1 cup broth a little at a time, continuing to stir, until a smooth béchamel sauce forms.

✤ When the rice is almost done, after about 16 minutes, add the béchamel sauce to the soup and continue to cook an additional 3 minutes or so, until thickened. Rice should be al dente, or firm to the bite; do not overcook.

✤ Season with salt and pepper and serve immediately.

SERVES 4
✤

Minestra di Riso e Pomodori

TOMATO-RICE SOUP

3 large tomatoes, peeled and sliced
5 cups Meat or Chicken Broth (pages
27 and 28), or 5 cups of water
plus 2 bouillon cubes and 1
tablespoon unsalted butter
½ cup Arborio rice
3 fresh basil leaves
Salt to taste

❧ Place the broth (or water, bouillon cubes, and butter) in a large stockpot and bring to a boil over high heat. Add the tomatoes and the rice, reduce the heat to medium, and simmer, checking the rice for doneness after about 16 minutes. Rice should be al dente, or firm to the bite; do not overcook.

❧ When the rice is done, add the basil. Taste for doneness and season with salt, if needed. Serve immediately.

SERVES 4
❧

Minestrina di Riso e Latte

MILK-RICE SOUP

When I was a child, this was the only soup I would voluntarily eat. Now I like to serve it as the first course of a light dinner, followed by vegetables and cheeses.

2½ quarts milk (whole, low-fat,
or skim)
1 cup Arborio rice
½ tablespoon lightly salted butter
Salt to taste

❧ Place the milk in a large stockpot and bring to a boil over medium heat.

❧ Add the rice and simmer, checking for doneness after about 16 minutes. Rice should be al dente, or firm to the bite; do not overcook.

❧ Add the butter and season with salt if needed. Serve immediately.

SERVES 4
❧

Minestra di Riso e Verdure

VEGETABLE-RICE SOUP

1 medium onion, peeled

3 medium carrots, peeled

2 medium turnips, peeled

3 tablespoons olive oil

1½ quarts Meat, Chicken, or Vegetable Broth (pages 27 to 29), or 1½ quarts water plus 2 bouillon cubes and 1 tablespoon unsalted butter

½ cup Arborio rice

Salt to taste

Freshly ground black pepper to taste

3 tablespoons chopped fresh parsley

Freshly grated Parmesan cheese

↜ Finely dice the onion, carrots, and turnips.

↜ Heat the olive oil in a large Dutch oven over medium heat. Add the vegetables and sauté until well coated with oil, about 1 minute.

↜ Add the broth (or water, bouillon cubes, and butter) and increase the heat to high. When the stock is boiling, add the rice, reduce the heat to medium, and simmer, checking the rice for doneness after about 16 minutes. Rice should be al dente, or firm to the bite; do not overcook.

↜ When the rice is done, season the soup with salt and pepper and stir in the parsley.

↜ Serve immediately, with Parmesan cheese at the table.

SERVES 4

↜

Minestrina di Riso al Limone

LEMON-RICE SOUP

5 cups Meat, Chicken, or Vegetable
    Broth (pages 27 to 29), or 5 cups
    water plus 2 bouillon cubes and
    1 tablespoon unsalted butter

½ cup Arborio rice

3 large eggs

Juice of 1 lemon

Salt to taste

⮞ Place the broth (or water, bouillon cubes, and butter) in a large stockpot and bring to a boil over high heat. Add the rice, reduce the heat to medium, and simmer, checking the rice for doneness after 16 minutes. Rice should be al dente, or firm to the bite; do not overcook.

⮞ Beat the eggs with the lemon juice and season lightly with salt.

⮞ When the rice is just done, stir the eggs into the soup and serve immediately.

SERVES 4

⮞

Minestrina di Riso e Fegatini di Pollo

RICE SOUP WITH
CHICKEN LIVERS

½ pound chicken livers

1 tablespoon unsalted butter

1½ quarts Meat, Chicken, or Vegetable Broth (pages 27 to 29), or 5 cups water plus 2 bouillon cubes and 1 tablespoon unsalted butter

1 cup Arborio rice

Salt to taste

Freshly ground black pepper to taste

2 tablespoons minced fresh parsley

Freshly grated Parmesan cheese

↔ Wash and dry the chicken livers and cut them into thin slices.

↔ Heat the butter in a large skillet over medium heat until foamy. Add the chicken livers and sauté until they lose their pink color, about 3 minutes.

↔ Place the broth (or water, bouillon cubes, and butter) in a large stockpot and bring to a boil over high heat. Add the rice, reduce the heat to medium, and simmer 12 minutes.

↔ Add the sautéed chicken livers to the broth, season with salt and pepper, and simmer an additional 4 minutes, checking the rice for doneness. Rice should be al dente, or firm to the bite; do not overcook.

↔ When the rice is done, stir in the parsley and serve immediately, with Parmesan cheese at the table.

SERVES 4

↔

Minestrone alla Milanese

Whereas in other regions of Italy they put pasta in their minestrone, in Milan we use rice. Another traditional Milanese ingredient is lard, but here I've used olive oil, which is more to my taste. Minestrone is equally good served hot, cold, or at room temperature. It is particularly delicious the next day.

3 tablespoons olive oil

½ garlic clove, minced

1 large onion, chopped

3 celery stalks, chopped

2 large tomatoes, peeled, seeded (see page 72), and chopped

2 medium potatoes, peeled and chopped

2 medium carrots, peeled and chopped

3 small zucchini, chopped

½ pound string beans, trimmed and chopped

1 cup shelled peas

1 cup finely chopped fresh parsley

2 cups dried black-eyed peas, soaked overnight (see Note)

1 cup coarsely chopped green cabbage

1½ cups Arborio rice

Freshly grated Parmesan cheese

✎ Heat the olive oil in a large stockpot, then add all the ingredients except the cabbage, rice, and Parmesan. Sauté for about 10 minutes. Add 2 quarts of water and bring to a boil, then lower the heat and simmer the soup for at least 2 hours.

✎ Add the cabbage and bring the soup back to a boil. Add the rice to the soup and boil for an additional 16 minutes. Serve with grated Parmesan cheese at the table.

NOTE: When using dried beans, pick them over carefully and discard any that look discolored. You should also stay away from beans that are over a year old. Place the beans in a large pot and add 1 teaspoon baking soda and lots of lukewarm water, since the beans will absorb water as they soak. Leave for 12 hours before using.

SERVES 6 TO 8

✎

*I*nsalate di Riso

HOT AND COLD
RICE SALADS

Rice Salad with Fruit and Cheese

Rice Salad with Tuna and Vegetables

Rice Salad with Tuna and Peas

Rice Salad with Tuna and Beans

Rice Salad with Tuna and Anchovies

Rice Salad with Shrimp

Rice Salad with Shrimp and Peas

*Rice Salad with Chicken
and Vegetables*

*Rice Salad with Onion, Black
Olives, and Fresh Tomatoes*

Rice Salad with String Beans

Rice Salad with Eggs and Bell Pepper

Rice Salad with Saffron

Piedmont-Style Rice Salad

Rice Salad with Mayonnaise

Cold Rice in Aspic

Hot Rice Salad

Bittersweet Rice Salad

*H*ot *summer days are meant to be spent outdoors as much as possible—reading a book in the shade of a tree, at the seashore, swimming, basking in the sun. In this mood of alternating indolence and activity, it is very hard to go into the kitchen and face slaving over the stove. Consider, instead, making one of these salads. They are the perfect vehicle for abundant summer fruits and vegetables. And they can be prepared quickly in the cool of the morning or evening, then kept in the refrigerator for as long as a day until you are ready to serve.*

You will notice that in many of these recipes I suggest putting the salad in a mold that will give the rice an attractive shape when served. This is really very easy to do, and you will find that this simple but elegant touch is much appreciated by your friends and family. The center of the ring mold also could be filled with crudités or, as the recipe for Insalata Fredda di Riso con Mayonnese *suggests, an appropriate dressing.*

Of course, you can enjoy cold rice salads in any season. In cold weather, you might want to serve a hot consommé afterward. Just don't forget the Milanese saying, "El ris el nass in l'acqua e el moeur in del vin (Rice grows in water and dies in wine)." *A nice cold bottle of dry white wine (or even a red) is always appropriate with these salads.*

Insalata di Riso con Frutta e Formaggio

RICE SALAD WITH FRUIT
AND CHEESE

This salad can really be a whole meal, served with a chilled bottle of Pinot Grigio and followed by a chocolate mousse.

2 cups Arborio rice

1 large tart apple (such as a Granny Smith), cut into bite-size pieces

6 pecan halves, coarsely chopped

4 ounces fontina or Swiss cheese, cut into bite-size pieces (about ½ cup)

5 ounces boiled ham, cut into bite-size pieces (about ½ cup)

3 tablespoons olive oil

Juice of 2 lemons

1 tablespoon Worcestershire sauce (optional)

Salt to taste

Freshly ground black pepper to taste

☙ Bring 2 quarts lightly salted water to a boil in a large saucepan. Add the rice and cook, checking for doneness after approximately 16 minutes. Rice should be al dente, or firm to the bite; do not overcook. When the rice is done, remove from the heat, pour into a colander, and rinse with cool water. Set the rice aside to drain and cool completely.

☙ When the rice has cooled, transfer to a large mixing bowl and add the apple, pecans, cheese, and ham. Gently stir to combine.

☙ Pour the olive oil, lemon juice, and Worcestershire sauce (if using) over the top and season to taste with salt and pepper. Stir again to thoroughly coat the rice with the dressing.

SERVES 4

☙

Riso in Insalata con Tonno e Verdure

RICE SALAD WITH TUNA AND VEGETABLES

2 cups Arborio rice

1 6½-ounce can water-packed tuna, drained

1 medium yellow bell pepper

2 medium tomatoes

3 hard-boiled eggs

6 ounces Swiss cheese

3 pitted black olives

3 pitted green olives

3 tablespoons olive oil

Juice of 3 lemons

4 tablespoons finely chopped fresh parsley

4 fresh basil leaves, finely chopped

Salt and freshly ground pepper to taste

Parsley sprigs, basil leaves, or other fresh herbs, for garnish

Sliced hard-boiled eggs, for garnish

✤ Bring 2 quarts lightly salted water to a boil in a large saucepan. Add the rice and cook, checking for doneness after approximately 16 minutes. Rice should be al dente, or firm to the bite; do not overcook. When the rice is done, remove from the heat, pour into a colander, and rinse with cool water. Set the rice aside to drain and cool completely.

✤ Meanwhile, cut the tuna, pepper, tomatoes, eggs, and cheese into bite-size chunks. Quarter the olives and set aside.

✤ When the rice is completely cooled, transfer to a large bowl and drizzle the olive oil and lemon juice over it. Add the tuna, vegetables, eggs, cheese, and herbs to the rice mixture and toss gently to combine. Season to taste with salt and pepper.

✤ Spoon the rice mixture into a 2-quart mold and chill for 1 hour before serving.

✤ To serve, submerge the mold up to the rim in hot water for 1 or 2 minutes, then remove from the water and invert onto a serving platter.

✤ Garnish with additional parsley and basil, and with sliced hard-boiled eggs, if desired.

SERVES 4

✤

Insalata di Riso con Tonno e Piselli

RICE SALAD WITH TUNA
AND PEAS

2 cups Arborio rice

2 cups shelled fresh peas, or 1
  10-ounce package frozen early
  peas

1 6½-ounce can water-packed tuna,
  drained and flaked

3 pitted green olives, minced

4 tablespoons olive oil, or more to taste

Juice of 2 lemons

Salt to taste

Freshly ground black pepper to taste

2 hard-boiled eggs, peeled and sliced,
  for garnish

✤ Bring 4 quarts lightly salted water to a boil in a large saucepan. Add the rice and cook, checking for doneness after approximately 16 minutes. Rice should be al dente, or firm to the bite; do not overcook. When the rice is done, remove from the heat, pour into a colander, and rinse with cool water. Set the rice aside to cool completely.

✤ Meanwhile, bring 1½ quarts lightly salted water to a boil in a saucepan. Add the fresh peas and cook until tender, 14 to 16 minutes. (Or cook the frozen peas according to the package directions.) Drain and set aside to cool.

✤ When both rice and peas are cool, combine in a large mixing bowl and add the tuna and olives. Pour the olive oil and lemon juice over all and toss well. Season with salt and pepper.

✤ Spoon the rice mixture into a 2-quart mold and refrigerate for at least 1 hour before serving.

✤ To serve, submerge the mold up to the rim in hot water for 1 or 2 minutes, then remove from the water and invert onto a serving platter.

✤ Garnish with the sliced hard-boiled eggs, if desired.

SERVES 4
✤

Insalata di Riso con Tonno e Fagioli

RICE SALAD WITH TUNA
AND BEANS

Even though this is a fish recipe, it is particularly robust. With a bottle of red wine like a Piedmontese Amarone, it makes a hearty lunch or dinner.

> *½ pound dried beans (such as*
> *cannellini), 2 cups shelled fresh,*
> *or 1 11-ounce can, drained*
> *2 cups Arborio rice*
> *1 large onion, peeled*
> *1 6½-ounce can water-packed tuna,*
> *drained and flaked*
> *1 celery stalk, finely chopped*
> *4 tablespoons olive oil*

✧ If using dried beans, soak them overnight in water to cover. Rinse and pick over the beans, then place them in a large saucepan with water to cover. Place the beans over high heat and bring to a boil. Reduce the heat and simmer gently until tender, about 1½ hours. (Or place beans in a covered saucepan with water to cover over high heat. Bring the water to a rapid boil, then remove the pan from the heat after 1 minute. Allow the beans to soak 45 minutes to 1 hour, then return to the heat and simmer until tender, about 1 hour.) If using fresh beans, bring 1 quart lightly salted water to a boil, add the beans, and simmer until tender, about 20 minutes. Drain the beans and allow to cool completely.

✧ Bring 4 quarts lightly salted water to a boil in a large saucepan. Add the rice and cook, checking for doneness after approximately 16 minutes. Rice should be al dente, or firm to the bite. When the rice is done, pour into a colander, and rinse with cool water. Set the rice aside to drain and cool completely.

✧ Place the onion in a medium saucepan with water to cover. Bring to a boil over high heat and simmer until tender but not mushy, about 12 minutes. Drain the onion and, when cool enough to handle, chop it fine.

✧ Combine the cooled beans, rice, onion, tuna, and celery in a mixing bowl. Pour the olive oil over the top and toss gently.

SERVES 4

✧

Insalata di Riso con Tonno e Acciughe

RICE SALAD WITH TUNA AND ANCHOVIES

2 cups Arborio rice

4 canned flat anchovy fillets, drained and minced

1 6½-ounce can water-packed tuna, drained and flaked

4 to 5 tablespoons olive oil, or more to taste

½ cup minced fresh parsley

↝ Bring 4 quarts lightly salted water to a boil in a large saucepan. Add the rice and cook, checking for doneness after approximately 16 minutes. Rice should be al dente, or firm to the bite; do not overcook. When the rice is done, remove from the heat, pour into a colander, and rinse with cool water. Set the rice aside to drain and cool completely.

↝ Combine the anchovies, tuna, olive oil, and parsley in a small saucepan over medium heat. Simmer gently 10 to 12 minutes, or until the sauce is well combined.

↝ Spread the cooled rice on a large serving platter and pour the hot sauce over it. Serve immediately.

SERVES 4

↝

Insalata di Riso con Gamberi

RICE SALAD WITH SHRIMP

2 cups Arborio rice

1 pound medium shrimp

2 medium cucumbers

2 hard-boiled eggs

2 medium tomatoes

3 tablespoons olive oil

Juice of 2 lemons

Salt to taste

Freshly ground black pepper to taste

⤙ Bring 4 quarts lightly salted water to a boil in a large saucepan. Add the rice and cook, checking for doneness after approximately 16 minutes. Rice should be al dente, or firm to the bite; do not overcook. When the rice is done, remove from the heat, pour into a colander, and rinse with cool water. Set the rice aside to drain and cool completely.

⤙ Meanwhile, bring 1½ quarts water to a boil in a large pan. Add the shrimp and cook until pink and just done, 5 to 6 minutes. Drain the shrimp and peel them when cool enough to handle.

⤙ Peel and thinly slice the cucumbers and the hard-boiled eggs. Halve and seed the tomatoes, then cut them into bite-size pieces.

⤙ When the rice is cool, gently stir in the shrimp, cucumbers, eggs, and tomatoes. Pour the olive oil and lemon juice over all, and toss gently to combine. Season with salt and pepper.

⤙ Spoon the rice mixture into a 2-quart mold and refrigerate for at least 1 hour before serving.

⤙ To serve, submerge the mold up to the rim in hot water for a minute or two, then remove from water and invert onto a serving platter.

SERVES 4
⤙

Insalata di Riso con Piselli e Gamberetti

RICE SALAD WITH SHRIMP
AND PEAS

2 cups Arborio rice

1½ pounds fresh medium shrimp

2 cups shelled fresh green peas, or
    1 10-ounce package frozen
    early peas

6 to 7 tablespoons olive oil

½ cup minced fresh parsley

Salt to taste

Freshly ground black pepper to taste

⊷ Bring 4 quarts lightly salted water to a boil in a large saucepan. Add the rice and cook, checking for doneness after approximately 16 minutes. Rice should be al dente, or firm to the bite; do not overcook. When the rice is done, remove from the heat, pour into a colander, and rinse with cool water. Set the rice aside to drain and cool completely.

⊷ Meanwhile, bring 2 quarts water to a boil in another large saucepan. Add the shrimp and cook until pink and just done, 5 to 6 minutes. Drain the shrimp and peel them when cool enough to handle.

⊷ In a medium saucepan, bring 1½ quarts lightly salted water to a boil. Add the fresh peas and cook until almost tender, 14 to 16 minutes. (Or, if using frozen peas, cook according to package directions.) Drain the peas and allow to cool.

⊷ When the rice, shrimp, and peas are cool, combine in a large bowl. Add the olive oil and parsley and toss gently. Season with salt and pepper.

⊷ Spoon the rice mixture into a 2-quart mold and refrigerate for at least 1 hour.

⊷ To serve, submerge the mold up to the rim in hot water for 1 or 2 minutes, then remove from the water and invert onto a serving platter.

SERVES 4

⊷

I serve this dish with a chilled Trementino, a white wine from Liguria.

Insalata di Riso con Pollo e Verdure

RICE SALAD WITH CHICKEN AND VEGETABLES

2 cups Arborio rice

2 cups shelled fresh peas, or 1
    10-ounce package frozen
    early peas

½ cup shredded cooked chicken

3 thick slices ham (about 7 ounces),
    julienned

4 pitted black olives, minced

4 fresh basil leaves, thinly sliced

4 to 5 tablespoons olive oil

2 tablespoons balsamic vinegar

Salt to taste

3 hard-boiled eggs, sliced, for garnish

↦ Bring 4 quarts lightly salted water to a boil in a large saucepan. Add the rice and cook, checking for doneness after approx-imately 16 minutes. Rice should be al dente, or firm to the bite; do not overcook. When the rice is done, remove from the heat, pour into a colander, and rinse with cool water. Set the rice aside to drain and cool completely.

↦ Meanwhile, bring 1 quart lightly salted water to a boil in a large saucepan. Add the fresh peas and cook until almost tender. (If using frozen peas, cook according to package directions.) Drain the peas and set aside to cool.

↦ Combine the cooled rice and peas, then add the chicken, ham, olives, and basil. Pour the olive oil and vinegar over the mix-ture, and toss thoroughly to combine. Season with salt.

↦ Spoon the rice mixture into a 2-quart mold and refrigerate for at least 1 hour.

↦ To serve, submerge the mold up to the rim in hot water for 1 or 2 minutes, then remove from the water and invert onto a serv-ing platter. Decorate the platter with the sliced hard-boiled eggs, if desired.

NOTE: This salad may be kept, refriger-ated, up to 24 hours. Unmold just before serving.

SERVES 4
↦

Insalata di Riso con Cipolla, Olive Nere, e Pomodoro Fresco

RICE SALAD WITH ONION, BLACK OLIVES, AND FRESH TOMATOES

2 cups Arborio rice

1 medium onion

2½ tablespoons olive oil

2 tablespoons red wine vinegar
or balsamic vinegar

1 teaspoon sugar

3 pitted black olives, minced

Salt to taste

Freshly ground black pepper to taste

3 medium tomatoes

4 fresh mint leaves, minced

⊷ Bring 4 quarts lightly salted water to a boil in a large pan. Add the rice and cook, checking for doneness after approximately 16 minutes. Rice should be al dente, or firm to the bite; do not overcook. When the rice is done, remove from the heat, pour into a colander, and rinse with cool water. Set the rice aside to drain and cool completely.

⊷ Meanwhile, slice the onion into thin rounds. In a large skillet over medium heat, warm the olive oil, then add the onion. Sauté gently until slightly softened, about 3 minutes.

⊷ Add the vinegar, sugar, olives, salt, and pepper and continue cooking until the onion is translucent, about 5 minutes. Set the onion sauce aside to cool.

⊷ Peel, seed, and coarsely chop the tomatoes (see page 72).

⊷ When the rice is completely cooled, place it in a large mixing bowl, add the onion sauce, and stir to combine. Place the tomatoes and mint on top of the rice mixture and toss gently.

SERVES 4

⊷

Insalata di Riso con Fagiolini

RICE SALAD WITH STRING BEANS

2 cups Arborio rice

1½ pounds fresh, very thin, string beans, or 1 9-ounce package frozen string beans

6 oil-cured black olives, pitted and minced

3 tablespoons olive oil

2 tablespoons red wine vinegar or balsamic vinegar, or more to taste

✦ Bring 4 quarts lightly salted water to a boil in a large saucepan. Add the rice and cook, checking for doneness after approximately 16 minutes. Rice should be al dente, or firm to the bite; do not overcook. When the rice is done, remove from the heat, pour into a colander, and rinse with cool water. Set the rice aside to drain and cool completely.

✦ If using fresh beans, wash them in cool water. Snap off the tops and bottoms of the beans to remove their strings, and break the beans into bite-size pieces.

✦ Bring 1½ quarts lightly salted water to a boil. Add the fresh beans and cook until tender, 15 to 20 minutes. (If using frozen beans, cook according to package directions.) Drain the beans, then set aside to cool.

✦ When the rice is cooled, stir in the beans and the olives.

✦ Combine the olive oil and vinegar, then pour over the rice mixture and toss gently.

SERVES 4
✦

Insalata di Riso con Uova e Peperoni Freschi

RICE SALAD WITH EGGS
AND BELL PEPPER

Potatoes and eggs, like potatoes and caviar, is a very special combination. This duo is often found in Spanish cooking, and I like to think this recipe derives from the Spanish domination of Italy.

2 cups Arborio rice

2 hard-boiled eggs

*1 medium potato, boiled until tender
    and peeled*

1 medium yellow or red bell pepper

4 pitted green olives

1 cup chopped fresh parsley

5 tablespoons ricotta cheese

3 tablespoons olive oil

*1 tablespoon red wine vinegar or
    balsamic vinegar, or more to taste*

Salt to taste

⊸ Bring 4 quarts lightly salted water to a boil in a large saucepan. Add the rice and cook, checking for doneness after approximately 16 minutes. Rice should be al dente, or firm to the bite; do not overcook. When the rice is done, remove from the heat, pour into a colander, and rinse with cool water. Set the rice aside to drain and cool completely.

⊸ Meanwhile, coarsely chop the eggs, potato, pepper, and olives.

⊸ When the rice is cool, stir in the chopped eggs, vegetables, olives, and parsley. Add the ricotta, olive oil, vinegar, and salt. Stir gently to combine, and adjust seasoning if necessary.

SERVES 4
⊸

Insalata di Riso con Zafferano

RICE SALAD WITH SAFFRON

2 cups Arborio rice

Large pinch of saffron

1½ tablespoons olive oil

2 cups shelled fresh peas, or 1
      10-ounce package frozen peas

2 small zucchini, halved lengthwise

2 medium carrots

Salt to taste

Freshly ground black pepper to taste

1 cup Homemade Mayonnaise
      (page 58)

5 whole fresh basil leaves, for garnish

↝ Bring 4 quarts lightly salted water to a boil in a large saucepan. Add the rice and cook, checking for doneness after approximately 16 minutes. Rice should be al dente, or firm to the bite; do not overcook. When the rice is done, remove from the heat, pour into a colander, and rinse with cool water. When drained, place the rice in a large mixing bowl, then stir in the saffron and olive oil. Set the rice aside to cool completely.

↝ Bring 1½ quarts water to a boil in a medium saucepan. Add the fresh peas and cook until almost tender, about 12 minutes. (If using frozen peas, follow the directions on the package.) Drain the peas and set aside.

↝ Steam the zucchini and the carrots until each is just tender, then coarsely chop them and add with the peas to the rice. Season with salt and pepper and toss well to mix.

↝ Spoon the rice into a 2-quart ring mold and press gently to set. Place the mold in the refrigerator and chill for at least 1 hour before serving.

↝ To serve, submerge the mold to the rim in hot water for 1 or 2 minutes, then remove from the water and invert onto a serving platter. Fill the center of the rice ring with the mayonnaise and decorate with the basil, if desired.

SERVES 4
↝

Insalata di Riso alla Piemontese

PIEDMONT-STYLE RICE
SALAD

The best truffles in Italy come from Alba, which is in the Piedmont.

2 cups Arborio rice

3 tablespoons olive oil

12 asparagus tips, trimmed

½ pound cultivated mushrooms

2 celery stalks

2 hard-boiled egg yolks

1 tablespoon Dijon mustard

Juice of 1 lemon

1 tablespoon heavy cream

1 tablespoon Marsala wine

Salt to taste

Freshly ground white pepper to taste

1 Alba Piemonte (white) truffle

↢ Bring 4 quarts lightly salted water to a boil in a large saucepan. Add the rice and cook, checking for doneness after 16 minutes. Rice should be al dente, or firm to the bite; do not overcook. When the rice is done, remove from the heat, pour into a colander, and rinse with cool water. When rice has drained, transfer to a mixing bowl and toss with 1½ tablespoons of the olive oil. Set aside to cool.

↢ Meanwhile, steam the asparagus until bright green and almost tender, from 10 to 25 minutes depending on their thickness. Set aside to cool.

↢ Clean the mushrooms and chop into bite-size pieces. Coarsely dice the celery.

↢ In a small mixing bowl, mash the egg yolks with a fork. Add the mustard, lemon juice, cream, Marsala, remaining 1½ tablespoons olive oil, salt, and pepper. Whisk thoroughly until well blended and creamy. Taste and adjust seasoning if necessary.

↢ Toss together the rice, asparagus, mushrooms, and celery. Add the dressing and toss again to coat thoroughly.

↢ Just before serving, grate a little truffle over each serving.

SERVES 4

↢

Insalata di Riso con Mayonnese

RICE SALAD WITH MAYONNAISE

2 cups Arborio rice

4 whole fresh artichokes, or 4 frozen
   artichoke hearts, thawed

6 medium cultivated mushrooms

2 tablespoons olive oil

3 tablespoons dry white wine

3 tablespoons minced fresh parsley

HOMEMADE MAYONNAISE

2 large egg yolks

1 teaspoon salt

1 cup olive oil, plus additional
   if needed

Juice of 1 lemon

Bring 4 quarts lightly salted water to a boil in a large saucepan. Add the rice and cook, checking for doneness after approximately 16 minutes. Rice should be al dente, or firm to the bite; do not overcook. When the rice is done, remove from the heat, pour into a colander, and rinse with cool water. Set aside the rice to drain and cool completely.

Place the fresh artichokes in a large saucepan with water to cover. Bring to a boil over high heat, then reduce the heat to medium-low and simmer until tender, 20 to 25 minutes. Drain the artichokes and allow to cool. Using a sharp knife, peel back the leaves and remove the hearts from the artichokes. Chop fresh or frozen artichoke hearts into bite-size pieces.

Clean the mushrooms and chop them into bite-size pieces.

Heat the olive oil in a large skillet over medium heat. Add the artichoke hearts and mushrooms and sauté until lightly golden, about 3 minutes. Add the wine and continue cooking until most of the wine has evaporated and the mushrooms are tender. Stir in the parsley and set aside.

Prepare the mayonnaise. Place the egg yolks in a medium mixing bowl with the salt. Whip together thoroughly with a balloon whisk until the eggs are lemon-colored and foamy. Whisking constantly, add the olive oil a drop at a time, gradually increasing the flow to a steady, thin stream. When all the olive oil has been incorporated (or when you have obtained the desired consistency), begin adding the lemon juice drop by drop, whisking all the while. The mayonnaise should have a soft, creamy consistency. Taste the mayonnaise for seasoning, whisking in more lemon juice, oil, or salt as needed.

⌁ Toss the sautéed vegetables with the cooled rice to combine. Add the mayonnaise and stir gently to coat.

⌁ Spoon the rice into a 2-quart ring mold, pressing gently to set. Refrigerate for at least 1 hour.

⌁ To serve, submerge the mold to the rim in hot water 1 or 2 minutes, then remove from the water and invert onto a serving platter.

S E R V E S   4
⌁

A dry white wine such as Verdicchio would be very appropriate with this salad.

Riso in Gelatina

C O L D   R I C E   I N   A S P I C

Beautiful and healthy, aspic has always been one of my favorite things. This dish may sound unfamiliar, but try it; it will surprise you.

1 medium yellow bell pepper

1 medium red bell pepper

1 envelope unflavored gelatin

2 cups water

1½ cups Marsala wine

2 cups Arborio rice

5 small fresh shrimp

1 hard-boiled egg, thinly sliced

15 pitted green olives, halved

1 6½-ounce can tuna in olive oil,
*   drained and flaked*

Juice of 1 lemon

Salt to taste

Freshly ground black pepper to taste

3 tablespoons olive oil

↪ Preheat the oven to 300°F. Cover a large baking sheet with aluminum foil.

↪ Wash the peppers, then halve them and remove the seeds. Cut each half into julienne. Spread the pepper strips over the baking sheet and roast in the oven until wilted, about 10 minutes. Remove from the oven and allow to cool.

↪ Dissolve the gelatin in the water and set aside to soften, about 10 minutes. Stir in the Marsala, then pour the mixture into a 2-quart mold. Place in the refrigerator to allow the aspic to harden a little bit.

↪ Bring 4 quarts lightly salted water to a boil in a large saucepan. Add the rice and cook, checking for doneness after approximately 16 minutes. Rice should be al dente, or firm to the bite; do not overcook. When the rice is done, remove from the heat, pour into a colander, and rinse with cool water. Set the rice aside to drain and cool completely.

↪ Meanwhile, bring 1 quart water to a boil in a medium saucepan. Add the shrimp and cook until pink and just done, about 4 minutes. Drain the shrimp, then peel them when cool enough to handle.

↪ Remove the aspic from the refrigerator. Place the egg slices on top of the aspic, along with the shrimp and olives, in an attractive pattern.

↬ Place the rice in a large mixing bowl and add the peppers, tuna, lemon juice, salt, pepper, and olive oil. Toss gently to combine. Spoon the rice on top of the aspic and press very gently into the mold. Refrigerate for at least 1 hour.

↬ To serve, submerge the mold up to the rim in hot water for 1 or 2 minutes, then remove from the water and invert onto a serving platter.

SERVES 4

↬

Insalata di Riso Calda

HOT RICE SALAD

2 cups Arborio rice
2 to 3 tablespoons olive oil
Juice of 2 lemons
½ cup minced fresh parsley

↬ Bring 4 quarts lightly salted water to a boil in a large saucepan. Add the rice and cook, checking for doneness after approximately 16 minutes. Rice should be al dente, or firm to the bite; do not overcook. When the rice is done, remove from the heat and pour into a colander. Toss and press down gently to remove excess water, then transfer the rice immediately to a large serving platter.

↬ Drizzle the olive oil and lemon juice over the hot rice and top with the parsley. Serve at once.

SERVES 4

↬

Insalata di Riso Agrodolce

BITTERSWEET RICE SALAD

This recipe is quite unusual in taste, but it's quite delicious, and I hope you will try it.

2 cups Arborio rice

5 tablespoons olive oil

2 large onions, minced

3 tablespoons red wine vinegar or
    balsamic vinegar

1 tablespoon sugar

Salt to taste

Freshly ground black pepper to taste

2 medium tomatoes, peeled, seeded,
    and coarsely chopped (see page
    72)

4 fresh mint leaves, for garnish

✧ Bring 2 quarts lightly salted water to a boil in a large saucepan. Add the rice and cook, checking for doneness after approximately 16 minutes. Rice should be al dente, or firm to the bite; do not overcook. When the rice is done, remove from the heat, pour into a colander, and rinse with cool water. Set the rice aside to drain and cool completely.

✧ Meanwhile, in a large skillet over medium heat, warm the olive oil, then add the onion. Sauté gently until the onion is softened, about 3 minutes. Stir in the vinegar, sugar, and salt and pepper to taste.

✧ Drain the tomatoes, then add them to the onions. Stir, and remove from the heat.

✧ When the rice is cooled, transfer to a large serving bowl and pour the onion-tomato mixture over the top. Stir gently to combine. Garnish the salad with the fresh mint leaves, if desired.

SERVES 4

✧

Risotti

Milanese-Style Risotto

Risotto with Osso Buco

Risotto with Garlic and Parsley

Risotto with Fresh Basil and Parsley

Risotto with Lemon

Risotto with Fresh Tomatoes and Basil

Risotto with Asparagus Tips

Risotto with Green and Red Peppers

Risotto with Peas

Anchovy-Mushroom Risotto

Risotto with Porcini Mushrooms

Milk Risotto

Gorgonzola Risotto

Risotto with Barolo Wine

Risotto with Raisins

White Wine Risotto with Truffles

Risotto with Champagne

Peasant-Style Risotto

Country-Style Risotto

Risotto with Shrimp

Risotto with Pancetta

Ham Risotto

Genoa-Style Risotto

Melon and Prosciutto Risotto

Chicken Risotto

Risotto with Quail

Seafood Risotto

Baked Risotto

Light Tomato Sauce

Black Risotto with Squid

Risotto with Sweet Italian Sausage

Risotto the Next Day

*R*isotto is a wonderful, delicious, and nutritious dish, although many people are intimidated by it and think of it as difficult to prepare. We Milanese usually serve risotto as a primo piatto, or first course, and follow it with a meat dish such as cotolette alla milanese *accompanied by vegetables, a salad of Boston lettuce or radicchio, roasted potatoes, cheese, and fruit.*

I'd like to lay to rest once and for all the notion that you need a Harvard degree in order to prepare a tasty, al dente risotto. Believe me, risotto is not at all difficult—provided, of course, that you follow a few simple rules:

1 ✣ Use only Arborio rice for risotto. Other types of rice do not absorb the large amount of broth and other liquids used to make risotto and will produce a soggy mess.

2 ✣ Do not overpower the rice with other ingredients; use only small amounts of butter, oil, or onion.

3 ✣ Use homemade broth whenever possible. If you don't have time to make your own broth, canned chicken broth (skimmed of excess fat, of course) will still produce a tasty risotto. Using reconstituted bouillon cubes will also make a satisfying risotto.

4 ✣ Stir risotto constantly, using a wooden spoon.

5 ✣ Do not overcook risotto. Frequent testing of rice grains as the risotto absorbs the cooking liquid is necessary to ensure that the rice is served al dente, or firm to the bite. In general, a finished risotto will take approximately eighteen minutes of cooking once you begin adding the broth, although the only way to tell for sure if the rice has reached the al dente stage and is ready to serve is by tasting as you go.

6 ⊷ Once the rice is al dente, serve the risotto immediately. Do not try to make the rice absorb any remaining liquids or hold the dish until guests arrive (some people do add butter at this stage, for a mantecato *finish or creamier texture, but it also makes for a heavier dish).*

7 ⊷ Start cooking the risotto only after all your guests have arrived. If you have prepared the vegetables, meats, or seafood ahead of time, a risotto takes only twenty minutes or so to prepare—time enough for your guests to greet each other and enjoy a drink before the risotto is served.

8 ⊷ Do not prepare a risotto for more than six people. If you are serving more than six at dinner, plan to make two individual risotti in separate cooking pots, even though this is more difficult because of the constant stirring required. You'll need to recruit a second person to help at the stove—but it also means your guests could enjoy two kinds of risotto: say, a classical Milanese risotto and a second made with vegetables, mushrooms, seafood, or even melon and prosciutto— whatever best complements the rest of the menu.

With these rules in mind, you're ready to make Northern Italy's classic first course.

Risotto alla Milanese

MILANESE-STYLE RISOTTO

Risotto alla Milanese always reminds me of the midnight suppers my mother would serve during World War II. Our family spent a few of the war years at our summer house in Finalpia, on the Italian Riviera. During nighttime air raids, we would spend the time in a natural cave, where we children were allowed to join the grown-ups for their midnight meal of Risotto alla Milanese. No artificial lights were permitted, so we dined by moonlight. It was romantic, and spooky, and delicious.

5 cups Chicken Broth (page 28)

2 tablespoons olive oil

1 small onion, minced

2 cups Arborio rice

1 large pinch of saffron

Salt to taste

Freshly ground black pepper to taste

1½ tablespoons unsalted butter or margarine

4 tablespoons freshly grated Parmesan cheese

↦ Place the broth in a covered saucepan over high heat. When the broth is hot but not yet simmering, reduce the heat to low.

↦ Place the olive oil in a large Dutch oven over medium heat. Add the onion and sauté gently until golden, about 3 minutes.

↦ Add the rice and stir 1 to 2 minutes, or until the rice is well coated with oil.

↦ Increase the heat to medium-high and add 1 cup of the hot broth, stirring constantly. When all of the broth has been absorbed by the rice, add another 1 cup broth and continue stirring.

↦ Sprinkle in the saffron. Repeat the process as necessary for 16 minutes, or until the rice is al dente, or firm to the bite. Taste, and season with salt and pepper if needed.

↦ Remove the risotto from the heat and stir in the butter and Parmesan cheese. Serve immediately.

SERVES 4
↦

A good bottle of Carema will enhance your Risotto alla Milanese.

Risotto all'Osso Buco

RISOTTO WITH OSSO
BUCO

Osso buco is as Milanese as il Duomo or la Madonnina. It is always served with Risotto alla Milanese.

6 1-inch-thick slices veal shank

4 tablespoons all-purpose flour

4 tablespoons olive oil

2 cups Meat Broth (page 27)

1½ cups dry white wine

Juice of 1 lemon

Risotto alla Milanese (page 67)

1 cup finely chopped fresh parsley

✤ Dredge both sides of the veal slices in the flour.

✤ Place the olive oil in a heavy skillet over medium heat. (The skillet should be large enough to hold the veal in a single layer.) When the oil is hot, carefully place the veal in the skillet and brown approximately 3 minutes on one side. Turn the veal and cook an additional 2 to 3 minutes on the second side, or until nicely browned.

✤ Add the broth and simmer until the liquid evaporates, then add the wine and a little more broth if necessary. Cover and simmer 12 to 14 minutes, or until the liquid is almost completely evaporated.

✤ Lower the heat and simmer very gently 10 minutes longer or until most of the liquid has evaporated, then add the lemon juice, remove the skillet from the heat, and set aside.

✤ Meanwhile, prepare the Risotto alla Milanese.

✤ Just before the risotto is done, return the veal to the stove and reheat. Sprinkle the parsley over the veal and serve the risotto hot, topped with the osso buco.

SERVES 4
✤

A bottle of Barbera goes well with the osso buco.

Risotto all'Aglio e Prezzemolo

RISOTTO WITH GARLIC AND PARSLEY

5 cups Chicken or Vegetable Broth
(pages 28 and 29)

2½ tablespoons olive oil

3 garlic cloves, finely chopped

2 cups Arborio rice

1 cup minced fresh parsley

4 tablespoons freshly grated Parmesan cheese

Salt to taste

Freshly ground black pepper to taste

↝ Place the broth in a covered medium saucepan over high heat. When the broth is hot but not yet simmering, reduce the heat to low.

↝ Place the olive oil in a large Dutch oven over medium heat. Add the garlic and sauté gently for 1 to 2 minutes, then add the rice and stir with a wooden spoon for 1 to 2 minutes, or until the rice is well coated with oil.

↝ Increase the heat to medium-high and add 1 cup of the hot broth, stirring constantly. When the rice has absorbed all the broth, add another 1 cup broth and continue stirring. Repeat the process as necessary for 16 minutes, or until the rice is al dente, or firm to the bite.

↝ When the rice is done, stir in the parsley and the Parmesan cheese (or, if you like, pass the cheese separately at the table). Taste, and add salt and pepper if needed.

↝ Remove the risotto from the heat and serve immediately.

SERVES 4

↝

Barbera wine is a must for this risotto.

Risotto con Basilico e Prezzemolo

RISOTTO WITH FRESH
BASIL AND PARSLEY

5 cups Meat, Chicken, or Vegetable
Broth (pages 27 to 29)

2 tablespoons olive oil

1 medium onion, minced

2 cups Arborio rice

½ cup minced fresh basil

½ cup minced fresh parsley

Salt to taste

Freshly ground black pepper to taste

½ cup freshly grated Parmesan cheese

↝ Place the broth in a covered medium saucepan over high heat. When the broth is hot but not yet simmering, reduce the heat to low.

↝ Place the olive oil in a large Dutch oven over medium heat. Add the onion and sauté gently until golden, about 3 minutes.

↝ Add the rice and stir with a wooden spoon for 1 to 2 minutes, or until the rice is well coated with oil.

↝ Increase the heat to medium-high and add 1 cup of the hot broth, stirring constantly. As the rice begins to absorb the last of the broth, add another 1 cup broth and continue stirring. Repeat the process as necessary for 15 to 18 minutes, or until the rice is al dente, or firm to the bite.

↝ Stir in the basil and parsley and taste. Season with salt and pepper if necessary.

↝ Stir in the Parmesan cheese or reserve to pass at the table. Remove the risotto from the heat and serve immediately.

SERVES 4

↝

This is a very delicate risotto. I would suggest a Corvo di Salaparuta as an accompaniment.

Risotto al Sugo di Limone

RISOTTO WITH LEMON

5 cups Meat Broth (page 27)
2 tablespoons unsalted butter
2 cups Arborio rice
Grated rind of 1 lemon
1 tablespoon all-purpose flour
Salt to taste
Freshly ground black pepper to taste
Juice of 1 lemon
5 tablespoons heavy cream

↫ Place the broth in a covered medium saucepan over high heat. When the broth is hot but not yet simmering, reduce the heat to low.

↫ Place 1 tablespoon of the butter in a large Dutch oven over medium heat. When the butter is foamy, add the rice and stir with a wooden spoon for 1 to 2 minutes, or until the rice is well coated with the butter.

↫ Increase the heat to medium-high and add ½ cup of the hot broth, stirring constantly. When the rice has absorbed most of the liquid, add another ½ cup broth and continue stirring. Repeat the process as necessary, and stir in the lemon rind after approximately 9 minutes. Continue cooking and stirring an additional 6 minutes, or until the rice is al dente, or firm to the bite. Set aside the risotto over very low heat to keep warm.

↫ Meanwhile, place the remaining 1 tablespoon butter in a small saucepan over medium heat. When the butter is foamy, add the flour and stir briskly until the butter is absorbed and the flour is lightly browned.

↫ Add the remaining broth to the flour and season with salt and pepper. Increase the heat to medium-high and bring the sauce mixture to a boil. After 2 minutes, remove the sauce from the heat and stir in the lemon juice and cream.

↫ Pour the sauce over the risotto, stir, and serve immediately.

SERVES 4
↫

I suggest a bottle of Soave with this dish (try one from Pieropan, Anselmi, or Masi).

Risotto con Pomodori Freschi e Basilico

RISOTTO WITH FRESH
TOMATOES AND BASIL

2 red (or 1 red and 1 yellow) bell
*   peppers*
Olive oil
Salt
1 pound fresh, ripe tomatoes (about
*   4 medium)*
4 cups Meat, Chicken, or Vegetable
*   Broth (pages 27 to 29)*
1 small onion, minced
2 cups Arborio rice
4 large, fresh basil leaves, chopped
4 tablespoons freshly grated
*   Parmesan cheese*

↭ Preheat the oven to 350°F. Line a large baking sheet with aluminum foil.

↭ Wash the peppers, then halve them and remove the seeds. Place the peppers cut side down on the baking sheet and drizzle with olive oil. Roast in the oven about 12 minutes, or until the peppers are wilted. Remove the peppers from the oven. When cool enough to handle, peel the pepper halves, sprinkle with salt, and set aside.

↭ Dip the tomatoes in boiling water for 1 minute, or until the skins begin to split. Remove the tomatoes from the water and allow to cool. Slip the skins off the tomatoes, then scoop out the seeds and coarsely chop the flesh. Set aside.

↭ Place the broth in a covered medium saucepan over high heat. When the broth is hot but not yet simmering, reduce the heat to low.

↭ Place 4 tablespoons olive oil in a large Dutch oven over medium heat. Add the onion and sauté gently until golden, about 3 minutes. Add the tomatoes and rice, and stir with a wooden spoon until well combined.

Increase the heat to high and add 1 cup of the hot broth, stirring constantly. When the rice has absorbed most of the broth, add another 1 cup broth and continue stirring. Repeat the process as necessary for approximately 16 minutes, then add the basil. Continue cooking and stirring about 1 minute longer, or until the rice is al dente, or firm to the bite.

Remove the risotto from the heat and pile the rice onto a warmed serving platter. Decorate the risotto with the roasted peppers and serve immediately with the Parmesan cheese.

SERVES 4

A light, dry white wine is best with this dish. Try an Orvieto Classico from Barbi, Antinori, or Barberani.

Risotto alle Punte di Asparago

RISOTTO WITH
ASPARAGUS TIPS

5 cups Chicken or Vegetable Broth
(pages 28 and 29)
2½ tablespoons olive oil
1 medium onion, minced
2 cups Arborio rice
16 fresh asparagus tips, washed
2½ tablespoons unsalted butter
1 cup freshly grated Parmesan cheese
Salt to taste
Freshly ground black pepper to taste

↦ Place the broth in a covered medium saucepan over high heat. When the broth is hot but not yet simmering, reduce the heat to low.

↦ Place the olive oil in a large Dutch oven over medium heat. Add the onion and sauté until golden, about 3 minutes.

↦ Add the rice and stir with a wooden spoon for 1 to 2 minutes, or until the rice is well coated with oil.

↦ Increase the heat to medium-high and add 1 cup of the hot broth, stirring constantly. When the rice has absorbed most of the liquid, add another 1 cup broth and continue stirring. Repeat as necessary.

↦ After 10 minutes, add the asparagus tips. Continue stirring and adding broth until the asparagus is tender and the rice is al dente, or firm to the bite—about 10 minutes longer.

↦ Remove the risotto from the heat and stir in the butter and Parmesan cheese. Taste, and add salt and pepper if necessary. Serve immediately.

SERVES 4
↦

The Chianti Ruffino produced by Tenuta Il Poggione and Fattoria di Vetrice are good choices with this risotto, as is Marchesi di Frescobaldi's Castello di Nipozzano.

Risotto con Peperoni

RISOTTO WITH GREEN
AND RED PEPPERS

1 large green bell pepper

1 large red bell pepper

5 cups water or Vegetable Broth

(page 29)

Pinch of saffron

4 tablespoons olive oil

1 small onion, minced

2 cups Arborio rice

Salt to taste

Freshly ground black pepper to taste

✦ Spear 1 pepper with a large roasting fork. Turn the pepper slowly over a medium gas flame until the skin is evenly charred. Set aside and repeat with the second pepper. Firmly brush off the charred pepper skins with a dish towel, then halve the peppers and remove the seeds. Cut each pepper half into julienne.

✦ Place the water or broth and the saffron in a covered medium saucepan over high heat. When the water is hot but not yet simmering, reduce the heat to low.

✦ Place the olive oil in a large Dutch oven over medium heat. Add the onion and sauté gently until golden, about 3 minutes.

✦ Add the rice, season with salt and pepper, and stir with a wooden spoon 1 to 2 minutes, until the rice is well coated with oil.

✦ Increase the heat to medium-high. Add the peppers and 1 cup of the hot saffron broth, stirring constantly. When all of the broth has been absorbed by the rice, add another 1 cup broth and continue stirring. Repeat the process as necessary for approximately 18 minutes, or until the rice is al dente, or firm to the bite.

✦ Remove the risotto from the heat and serve immediately.

SERVES 4

✦

The hearty flavors of this risotto call for a robust wine; you might try a Barbera from the Piedmont region.

Risotto con i Piselli

RISOTTO WITH PEAS

6 cups Meat, Chicken, or Vegetable
    Broth (pages 27 to 29)
2 tablespoons olive oil
1 small onion, minced
1½ cups shelled fresh peas, or 1
    10-ounce package frozen peas
1 medium tomato, peeled, seeded,
    and cut into small pieces (see
    page 72), or 1 small peeled
    canned tomato
2 cups Arborio rice
Salt to taste
½ tablespoon unsalted butter
1 cup freshly grated Parmesan cheese

↩ Place the broth in a covered medium saucepan over high heat. When the broth is hot but not yet simmering, reduce the heat to low.

↩ Place the olive oil in a large Dutch oven over medium heat. Add the onion and sauté gently until golden, about 3 minutes.

↩ Add the peas, tomato, and ½ cup of the hot broth. Simmer gently until the broth is almost evaporated.

↩ Add the rice, season with salt, and increase the heat to medium-high. Add 1 cup hot broth, stirring constantly with a wooden spoon. When the rice has absorbed most of the broth, add another 1 cup broth and continue stirring. Repeat as necessary for 16 to 18 minutes, or until the rice is al dente, or firm to the bite.

↩ Add the butter and stir. Remove the risotto from the heat and serve immediately. Pass the Parmesan cheese at the table.

SERVES 4

↩

I would suggest a special white wine made in the Piedmont from Arneis grapes by Ceretto or Giacosa.

Risotto alle Acciughe e Funghi

ANCHOVY-MUSHROOM
RISOTTO

*1½ ounces dried porcini mushrooms,
  or 1 pound sliced fresh porcini
  mushrooms (see page 17)*

5 cups Chicken Broth (page 28)

3 tablespoons olive oil

1 garlic clove

1½-ounce can anchovy fillets, chopped

2 cups Arborio rice

*½ pound fresh chicken livers, cut
  into bite-size pieces*

↬ Place the dried mushrooms in a small bowl with hot water to cover. Let stand at least 30 minutes. Drain the mushrooms and wash them well to remove all traces of dirt and sand. Cut the mushrooms into bite-size pieces and place in a bowl with more hot water. Let stand until ready to use.

↬ Place the broth in a covered medium saucepan over high heat. When the broth is hot but not yet boiling, reduce the heat to low.

↬ Place the olive oil and the garlic in a large Dutch oven over medium heat.

↬ Drain the mushrooms and squeeze them to remove excess water.

↬ When the oil begins to sizzle, remove the garlic and add the mushrooms, anchovies, and rice. Stir with a wooden spoon for 1 to 2 minutes, or until the rice is well coated.

↬ Increase the heat to medium-high and add 1 cup of the hot broth, stirring constantly. When the rice has absorbed most of the liquid, add another 1 cup broth and continue stirring. Repeat as necessary.

↬ After 10 minutes, add the chicken livers. Continue adding broth and stirring until the chicken livers lose their pink color and the rice is al dente, or firm to the bite—about 8 minutes longer.

↬ Remove the risotto from the heat and serve immediately.

SERVES 4
↬

This strong-flavored risotto calls for an assertive red wine. I suggest Nebbiolo d'Alba from Angelo Gaja, Bruno Giacosa, or Alfredo Prunotto.

Risotto con Funghi Porcini

RISOTTO WITH PORCINI MUSHROOMS

1½ ounces dried porcini mushrooms,
*   or 1 pound sliced fresh porcini*
*   mushrooms (see page 17)*
5 cups Chicken Broth (page 28)
2½ tablespoons olive oil
1 medium onion, minced
2 cups Arborio rice
2 tablespoons unsalted butter
3 tablespoons freshly grated Parmesan
*   cheese*
Salt to taste
Freshly ground black pepper to taste

↦ If you are using dried mushrooms, place them in a small bowl with hot water to cover. Let stand at least 30 minutes. Drain the mushrooms and wash them well to remove any traces of sand or dirt. Squeeze the mushrooms to remove excess water and set aside.

↦ Place the broth in a covered saucepan over high heat. When the broth is hot but not yet simmering, reduce the heat to low.

↦ Place the olive oil in a large Dutch oven over medium heat. Add the onion and sauté gently until golden, about 3 minutes.

↦ Add the rice and stir with a wooden spoon for 1 to 2 minutes, or until the rice is well coated with oil.

↦ Increase the heat to medium-high and add 1 cup of the hot broth, stirring constantly. When the rice has absorbed most of the liquid, add another 1 cup broth and continue stirring. Repeat the process as necessary.

↦ After 10 minutes, add the mushrooms. Continue adding broth and stirring until the rice is al dente, or firm to the bite—about 8 minutes longer.

↦ Remove the risotto from the heat and stir in the butter, if desired, and the Parmesan cheese. Taste, and add salt and pepper if needed. Serve immediately.

SERVES 4
↦

Brunello di Montalcino, particularly those produced by Banfi, Biondi-Santi, San Felice, and Col d'Orcia, is a wonderful, compactly textured wine to serve with this dish.

Risotto al Latte

MILK RISOTTO

4 cups milk

1 teaspoon salt

2 cups Arborio rice

1½ tablespoons unsalted butter

½ cup freshly grated Parmesan cheese

↦ Place the milk and salt in a large saucepan and bring to a boil over high heat.

↦ Add the rice, reduce the heat to medium-low, and simmer, stirring occasionally, for approximately 16 minutes, or until the milk has been absorbed and the rice is al dente, or firm to the bite. (If the rice becomes too dry, add more milk to moisten.)

↦ Remove the risotto from the heat and stir in the butter and Parmesan cheese. Serve immediately.

SERVES 4
↦

Risotto al Gorgonzola

GORGONZOLA RISOTTO

Italy's most famous "blue" cheese is named after the small village in Lombardy where it has been made for centuries.

5 cups Meat Broth (page 27)

1½ tablespoons unsalted butter

3 tablespoons olive oil

1 small onion, minced

2 cups Arborio rice

½ pound (about 1½ cups) Gorgonzola
    cheese, crumbled

Salt to taste

Freshly ground black pepper to taste

1 cup freshly grated Parmesan cheese
    (optional; see Note)

✧ Place the broth in a covered medium saucepan over high heat. When the broth is hot but not yet simmering, reduce the heat to low.

✧ Place the butter and olive oil in a large Dutch oven over medium heat. When the but-ter is foamy, add the onion and sauté gently until golden, about 3 minutes.

✧ Add the rice and stir with a wooden spoon for 1 to 2 minutes, or until the grains are well coated with oil.

✧ Increase the heat to medium-high and add 1 cup of the hot broth, stirring constantly. When all the broth has been absorbed by the rice, add another 1 cup broth and continue stirring. Repeat the process as necessary for 15 to 16 minutes, or until the rice is almost al dente, or firm to the bite.

✧ Add the Gorgonzola and continue stir-ring 1 to 2 minutes or until the cheese is melted and thoroughly incorporated into the rice.

✧ Remove the risotto from the heat, sea-son with salt and pepper, and serve imme-diately. Pass the Parmesan cheese at the table.

NOTE: Some people love the taste of Parmesan cheese with Gorgonzola, and oth-ers prefer their Gorgonzola solo. Let each diner be the judge.

SERVES 4

✧

Chianti Classico da Pasto is a good choice with this risotto.

Risotto al Barolo

RISOTTO WITH BAROLO
WINE

5 cups Meat Broth (page 27)

2 tablespoons olive oil

1 small onion, minced

2 cups Arborio rice

1½ cups Barolo wine

1 tablespoon unsalted butter or
   margarine

4 tablespoons freshly grated Parmesan
   cheese

Salt to taste

Freshly ground black pepper to taste

⟿ Place the broth in a covered medium saucepan over high heat. When the broth is hot but not yet simmering, reduce the heat to low.

⟿ Place the olive oil in a large Dutch oven over medium heat. Add the onion and sauté gently until golden, about 3 minutes.

⟿ Add the rice and stir with a wooden spoon for 1 to 2 minutes, or until the rice is well coated with oil.

⟿ Increase the heat to medium-high and add 1 cup of the hot broth, stirring constantly. When the rice has absorbed most of the liquid, add another 1 cup broth and continue stirring. Repeat the process, adding cupfuls of broth—and also incorporating 1 cup of the wine—for approximately 16 minutes, or until the rice is al dente, or firm to the bite.

⟿ Stir in the butter, then the remaining ½ cup wine and the Parmesan cheese. Taste, and add salt and pepper if needed. Remove the risotto from the heat and serve immediately.

SERVES 4
⟿

With this dish you want the perfect Barolo, preferably the one you used to make the risotto. Look for one produced by Ceretto, Giacosa, Vietti, or Prunotto.

Risotto all'Uvetta Passita

RISOTTO WITH RAISINS

In Tuscany it is not uncommon to encounter raisins in a savory main dish.

3 tablespoons raisins

1 cup warm water

1 quart Meat Broth (page 27)

3 tablespoons olive oil

1 small garlic clove

½ cup finely chopped fresh parsley

2 cups Arborio rice

Salt to taste

½ cup freshly grated Parmesan cheese

❧ Place the raisins and warm water in a small bowl and let stand at least 30 minutes.

❧ Place the broth in a medium covered saucepan over high heat. When the broth is hot but not yet simmering, reduce the heat to low.

❧ Place the olive oil in a large Dutch oven over medium heat. Add the garlic and the parsley, and sauté gently 1 to 2 minutes, or until the garlic begins to turn golden. Remove the garlic.

❧ Add the rice and stir with a wooden spoon for 1 to 2 minutes, until the grains are well coated with oil.

❧ Meanwhile, drain the raisins and squeeze to remove excess water.

❧ Increase the heat to medium-high and add 1 cup of the hot broth. Stir the rice constantly and as soon as the liquid is absorbed, add an additional 1 cup broth and continue stirring. Repeat as necessary for 14 to 15 minutes, or until the rice is al dente, or firm to the bite. Add salt to taste.

❧ Remove the risotto from the heat, stir in the raisins and the Parmesan cheese, and serve immediately.

SERVES 4

❧

This risotto is great with a dry white wine such as Orvieto Classico. Orvieto, from Umbria, is a blend of several grape varieties. Producers to look for include Antinori, Barbi, Barberani, and Bigi.

Risotto al Vino Bianco con Tartufo

WHITE WINE RISOTTO WITH TRUFFLES

Truffles are really the best thing that could happen to your risotto, so even though they're expensive, try them at least once.

5 cups Chicken Broth (page 28)

2½ tablespoons unsalted butter

1 medium onion, minced

2 cups Arborio rice

2 cups very dry white wine

1 small white truffle

1 cup freshly grated Parmesan cheese

⊸ Place the broth in a covered medium saucepan over high heat. When the broth is hot but not yet simmering, reduce the heat to low.

⊸ Place 1 tablespoon of the butter in a large Dutch oven over medium heat. When the butter is foamy, add the onion and sauté gently until golden, about 3 minutes.

⊸ Add the rice and stir with a wooden spoon for 1 to 2 minutes, or until the rice is well coated with oil.

⊸ Increase the heat to medium-high and add 1 cup of the hot broth, stirring constantly. When the rice has absorbed most of the liquid, add another 1 cup broth and continue stirring. Repeat the process as necessary for 16 minutes, or until the rice is al dente, or firm to the bite. Add the wine and stir.

⊸ Remove the risotto from the heat and stir in the remaining 1½ tablespoons butter. Serve immediately, with a little truffle grated over each portion. Top with Parmesan cheese if desired.

SERVES 4

⊸

It's not necessary to serve the same wine you used to make this recipe. The most important thing is to serve a very special wine since this is a very special risotto. A Pinot Grigio of Friuli would be an excellent choice.

Risotto allo Champagne

RISOTTO WITH CHAMPAGNE

3 cups Meat Broth (page 27)

1½ tablespoons unsalted butter

1 small onion, minced

2 cups Arborio rice

½ bottle Champagne, preferably dry
    or brut, at room temperature

½ cup heavy cream

5 tablespoons freshly grated Parmesan
    cheese

Salt to taste

↪ Place the broth in a small covered saucepan over high heat. When the broth is hot but not yet simmering, reduce the heat to low.

↪ Place the butter in a large Dutch oven over medium heat. When the butter is foamy, add the onion and sauté gently until golden, about 3 minutes.

↪ Add the rice and stir with a wooden spoon for 1 to 2 minutes until the rice is well coated with butter.

↪ Increase the heat to medium-high and add 1 cup Champagne, stirring constantly. When the rice has absorbed most of the Champagne, add 1 cup of the hot broth and continue stirring. Repeat the process, alternating Champagne and broth, for approximately 15 minutes.

↪ Meanwhile, place the cream in a small saucepan over low heat and warm gently.

↪ When the rice is just short of al dente (tender, but still firm to the bite), stir in the cream and the Parmesan cheese. Taste, and add salt if needed.

↪ Remove the risotto from the heat and serve immediately.

SERVES 4
↪

A special Champagne should be served with this very special risotto.

Risotto alla Contadina

PEASANT-STYLE RISOTTO

5 cups Meat, Chicken or Vegetable
    Broth (pages 27 to 29)
2 tablespoons olive oil
1 medium carrot, finely chopped
1 celery stalk, finely chopped
1 small onion, minced
1 salsiccia or sweet Italian sausage
    (about 5 ounces), cut into
    bite-size pieces
2 cups Arborio rice
1 tablespoon unsalted butter
1 cup freshly grated Parmesan cheese

⟜ Place the broth in a covered medium saucepan over high heat. When the broth is hot but not yet simmering, reduce the heat to low.

⟜ Place the olive oil in a large Dutch oven over medium heat. Add the carrot, celery, onion, and *salsiccia* and sauté gently until the onion is golden, about 3 minutes. Pour off any excess fat released by the *salsiccia*.

⟜ Add the rice and stir with a wooden spoon for 1 to 2 minutes or until the rice is well coated with oil.

⟜ Increase the heat to medium-high and add 1 cup of the hot broth, stirring constantly. When the rice has absorbed most of the liquid, add another 1 cup broth and continue stirring. Repeat as necessary for approximately 16 minutes, or until the rice is al dente, or firm to the bite.

⟜ Remove the risotto from the heat and stir in the butter and the Parmesan cheese. Serve immediately.

SERVES 4
⟜

I think you'll find Barolo (try Ceretto, Giacosa, Prunotto, or Pio Cesare) a good match here.

Risotto alla Campagnola

COUNTRY-STYLE RISOTTO

4 cups Chicken or Vegetable Broth
(pages 28 and 29)
2½ tablespoons olive oil
1 medium onion, minced
1 medium carrot, finely chopped
2 cups shelled fresh or frozen peas
1 cup finely chopped celery
3 medium zucchini, finely chopped
2 cups Arborio rice
2 tablespoons unsalted butter
1 cup freshly grated Parmesan cheese

✤ Place the broth in a covered medium saucepan over high heat. When the broth is hot but not yet simmering, reduce the heat to low.

✤ Place the olive oil in a large Dutch oven over medium heat and add the onion. Sauté gently until golden, about 3 minutes, then add the carrot, peas, celery, and zucchini and sauté an additional 2 to 3 minutes, or until the vegetables are wilted.

✤ Stir in the rice and stir with a wooden spoon for 1 to 2 minutes, or until the rice is well coated with oil.

✤ Increase the heat to medium-high, then add 1 cup of the hot broth, stirring constantly. After 5 to 7 minutes, when the rice has absorbed most of the liquid, add another 1 cup broth and continue stirring. Repeat the process as necessary for 11 to 13 minutes longer, or until the rice is al dente, or firm to the bite.

✤ Remove the risotto from the heat and stir in the butter and Parmesan cheese. Serve immediately.

SERVES 4
✤

A bottle of Dolcetto (from Marcarini, Giacosa, or Mascarello) is a delicious accompaniment to this dish.

Risotto ai Gamberetti

RISOTTO WITH SHRIMP

20 small fresh shrimp (about 1½
   pounds)
4 cups Fish Broth (page 30)
3 tablespoons olive oil
1 medium onion, minced
2 cups Arborio rice
2 cups dry white wine
2 tablespoons unsalted butter
1 cup freshly grated Parmesan cheese
Salt to taste
Freshly ground black pepper to taste

↬ Bring 2 quarts water to a boil in a large saucepan. Add the shrimp and cook until pink and just barely done, about 3 minutes. Remove the shrimp from the heat, drain, and allow to cool. Peel the shrimp and set aside.

↬ Place the broth in a covered medium saucepan over high heat. When the broth is hot but not yet simmering, reduce the heat to low.

↬ Place the olive oil in a large Dutch oven over medium heat. Add the onion and sauté until golden, about 3 minutes.

↬ Add the rice and stir with a wooden spoon for 1 to 2 minutes, or until the rice is well coated with oil.

↬ Increase the heat to medium-high and add 1 cup of the hot broth, stirring constantly. When the rice has absorbed most of the liquid, add another 1 cup broth and continue stirring. Repeat the process as necessary.

↬ After 15 minutes, add the wine and the shrimp. Continue stirring and, when the wine has been absorbed, add broth for approximately 5 minutes longer, or until the rice is al dente, or firm to the bite.

↬ Remove the rice from the heat and stir in the butter and Parmesan cheese. Taste, and add salt and pepper if needed. Serve immediately.

SERVES 4

↬

The Verdicchio di Matelica from the Marche region near Ancona and Ascoli Piceno is a good complement to this risotto. Reliable producers are Azienda Agricola Maltei and Cooperativa Enopolio di Matelica. Verdicchio should be served chilled.

Risotto alla Pancetta

RISOTTO WITH PANCETTA

Pancetta is the same cut of pork we call bacon—although only pancetta *affumicata* is smoked like bacon—and it gets its name from its place of origin: the *pancia*—belly—of the pig.

> 5 cups Chicken Broth (page 28)
>
> 4 ounces unsmoked pancetta
>
> ½ tablespoon unsalted butter
>
> 1 small onion, minced
>
> 2 cups Arborio rice
>
> ½ cup heavy cream
>
> Salt to taste
>
> Freshly ground black pepper to taste
>
> 1 cup freshly grated Parmesan cheese

⊷ Place the broth in a covered medium saucepan over high heat. When the broth is hot but not yet simmering, reduce the heat to low.

⊷ Finely dice the pancetta.

⊷ Place the butter in a large Dutch oven over medium heat. When the butter is foamy, add the pancetta and the onion and sauté gently until the pancetta loses its pink color and the onion is golden, about 3 minutes.

⊷ Add the rice and stir with a wooden spoon for 1 to 2 minutes, or until the rice is well coated with butter.

⊷ Increase the heat to medium-high and add 1 cup of the hot broth, stirring constantly. When the rice has absorbed most of the liquid, add another 1 cup broth and continue stirring. Repeat the process as necessary for approximately 16 minutes, or until the rice is al dente, or firm to the bite.

⊷ Add the cream and stir to combine. Taste, and add salt and pepper if needed.

⊷ Remove the risotto from the heat and serve immediately, with the Parmesan cheese on the side.

SERVES 4

⊷

Choose a bottle of Barbaresco, which complements the rich pancetta, to accompany this *primo piatto*. Producers to look for include Gaja, Ceretto, and Bruno Giacosa.

Risotto al Prosciutto Cotto

H A M   R I S O T T O

2 ounces dried porcini mushrooms

2 cups warm water

5 cups Meat, Chicken or Vegetable
    Broth (pages 27 to 29)

2 tablespoons unsalted butter

2 tablespoons olive oil

1 small onion, minced

2 cups Arborio rice

Salt to taste

Freshly ground black pepper to taste

1½ cups dry white wine

4 ounces cooked ham, cubed (about
    ½ cup)

½ cup light cream

1 cup freshly grated Parmesan cheese

✧ Place the dried mushrooms in a small bowl with the water and let stand at least 1 hour. Drain the mushrooms and wash thoroughly under cold running water to remove any sand or particles of dirt. Set aside.

✧ Place the broth in a covered saucepan over high heat. When the broth is hot but not yet simmering, reduce the heat to low.

✧ Place the butter and olive oil in a large Dutch oven over medium heat. When the butter is foamy, add the onion and sauté gently until golden, about 3 minutes.

✧ Add the rice, season with salt and pepper, and stir with a wooden spoon for 1 to 2 minutes, or until the grains are well coated.

✧ Add the wine and stir constantly until absorbed.

✧ Increase the heat to medium-high and add 1 cup of the hot broth, stirring constantly. When all of the broth has been absorbed by the rice, add another 1 cup broth and continue stirring. Add the mushrooms and continue adding broth as necessary for about 18 minutes, stirring all the while, until the rice is al dente, or firm to the bite.

✧ Remove the risotto from the stove and stir in the ham and cream. Stir in the Parmesan cheese (or, if you like, reserve the Parmesan to pass at the table). Serve immediately.

S E R V E S   4
✧

Risotto alla Genovese

GENOA-STYLE RISOTTO

5 cups Meat Broth (page 27)

4 tablespoons olive oil

1 small onion, minced

4 tablespoons minced fresh parsley

½ pound lean ground veal

2 cups Arborio rice

½ cup freshly grated Parmesan cheese

Salt to taste

❧ Place the broth in a covered medium saucepan over high heat. When the broth is hot but not yet simmering, reduce the heat to low.

❧ Place the olive oil in a large Dutch oven over medium heat. Add the onion, parsley, and veal and sauté gently until the onion is wilted and beginning to turn golden and the veal has lost its pink color.

❧ Add the rice and stir with a wooden spoon for 1 to 2 minutes, or until the rice is well coated with oil.

❧ Increase the heat to medium-high and add 1 cup of the hot broth, stirring constantly. When the rice has absorbed most of the liquid, add an additional 1 cup broth and continue stirring. Repeat the process as necessary for approximately 16 minutes, or until the rice is al dente, or firm to the bite.

❧ Remove the risotto from the heat and stir in the Parmesan cheese. Taste, and season with salt if necessary. Serve immediately.

SERVES 4

❧

A red wine such as Chianti would go well with this risotto.

Risotto con Prosciutto e Melone

MELON AND PROSCIUTTO
RISOTTO

1 large honeydew melon

1 quart Meat Broth (page 27)

5 tablespoons unsalted butter

1 small onion, minced

2 cups Arborio rice

1½ cups dry white wine

1 cup light cream

½ cup (about 4 ounces) thinly sliced
*   prosciutto*

Salt to taste

Freshly ground black pepper to taste

1 cup freshly grated Parmesan cheese

✧ Halve the melon and remove the seeds. Cut the flesh into small cubes and place in the work bowl of a food processor fitted with the metal blade. Lightly puree the melon and set aside.

✧ Place the broth in a covered saucepan over high heat. When the broth is hot but not yet simmering, reduce the heat to low.

✧ Place the butter in a large Dutch oven over medium heat. Add the onion and sauté until golden, about 3 minutes.

✧ Add the rice and stir with a wooden spoon for 1 to 2 minutes, or until the rice is well coated with butter. Add the wine a little at a time, stirring constantly until the rice has absorbed the liquid.

✧ Increase the heat to medium-high, add ½ cup of the hot broth, and continue stirring. When the liquid has been absorbed, add another ½ cup broth and continue stirring. Repeat the process as necessary for approximately 16 minutes, or until the rice is al dente, or firm to the bite.

✧ Add the melon puree, cream, and prosciutto and quickly stir into the rice. Taste, and season with salt and pepper if necessary.

✧ Remove the risotto from the heat and serve immediately. Pass the Parmesan cheese at the table if desired.

SERVES 4
✧

Risotto al Pollo

CHICKEN RISOTTO

CHICKEN BROTH (see Note)

1 medium chicken (about 2½ pounds)

1 large carrot

1 celery stalk

2 tablespoons olive oil

1 medium onion, minced

1½ cups dry white wine

2 medium tomatoes, peeled, seeded,
      and coarsely chopped (see page
      72), or 1 16-ounce can peeled
      Italian plum tomatoes, chopped

2 cups Arborio rice

Salt to taste

Freshly ground black pepper to taste

1 cup freshly grated Parmesan cheese

❧ Prepare the chicken broth. Place the chicken in a large Dutch oven with water to cover. Bring to a boil over high heat, cover, and reduce the heat to medium-low. Simmer the chicken until the meat is tender and beginning to fall away from the bone.

❧ Carefully lift the chicken from the pot and onto a large platter. When the chicken is cool enough to handle, remove the meat from the bones, discarding the skin. Reserve the chicken meat and return the carcass to the pot with the cooking liquid.

❧ Add the carrot and celery to the pot, add enough water to cover, and return to a boil. Reduce the heat to low and allow the broth to simmer very slowly, with only an occasional bubble breaking the surface, for about 2½ hours. Skim foam from the surface from time to time.

❧ Remove the vegetables and chicken carcass from the pot. Strain the broth through a fine linen towel or double thickness of cheesecloth and refrigerate. When broth is chilled, skim any solidified fat from the surface. You should have 3 to 4 quarts of broth.

❧ Meanwhile, cut the reserved chicken into bite-size pieces.

❧ Place 5 cups of the broth in a covered medium saucepan over high heat. (Reserve the remaining broth for another use.) When the broth is hot but not yet simmering, reduce the heat to low.

❧ Warm the olive oil in a large skillet over medium heat. Add the onion and sauté gently until the onion begins to turn golden, about 3 minutes. Add the chicken and sauté 2 minutes longer.

✣ Pour the wine over the chicken and continue cooking. Meanwhile, drain the tomatoes. When the wine has evaporated, add the tomatoes to the skillet and then add the rice. Stir with a wooden spoon for 1 to 2 minutes or until the rice is well coated with the chicken mixture.

✣ Increase the heat to medium-high and add 1 cup of the hot broth, stirring constantly. When all of the broth has been absorbed by the rice, add another 1 cup broth and continue stirring. Repeat the process as necessary for 16 minutes, or until the rice is done—al dente, or firm to the bite.

✣ Remove the risotto from the heat and season with salt and pepper. Stir in the Parmesan cheese and serve immediately.

NOTE: Leftover broth will keep in the refrigerator about 5 days or may be frozen for up to 1 month.

SERVES 4
✣

I recommend Pinot Grigio to accompany this risotto, since it is fruity and somewhat spicy—a good complement to the chicken. I think you will be pleased with the wines produced by Brigl, Boscaini, and Banfi.

Risotto con le Quaglie

RISOTTO WITH QUAIL

4 quail

Salt

4 thin slices unsmoked pancetta

1½ cups dry white wine

5 cups Meat Broth (page 27)

1½ tablespoons unsalted butter or margarine

1 small onion, minced

2 cups Arborio rice

Salt to taste

Freshly ground black pepper to taste

1 cup freshly grated Parmesan cheese

✛ Wash the quail and pat them dry with a clean dish towel. Sprinkle each quail with salt and wrap with a slice of pancetta. Secure the pancetta with toothpicks.

✛ Place the quail in a large, heavy skillet over medium-low heat and sauté 15 minutes, turning occasionally to brown each bird evenly. Add the wine and simmer until most of the liquid evaporates, about 3 minutes.

✛ Place the broth in a covered saucepan over high heat. When the broth is hot but not yet simmering, reduce the heat to low.

✛ Place 1 tablespoon of butter in a large Dutch oven over medium heat. Add the onion and sauté until golden, about 3 minutes.

✛ Add the rice and stir with a wooden spoon for 1 to 2 minutes, or until the rice is well coated with butter.

✛ Increase the heat to medium-high and add 1 cup of the hot broth, stirring constantly. When the rice has absorbed most of the liquid, add another 1 cup broth and continue stirring. Repeat the process as necessary for approximately 16 minutes, or until the rice is al dente, or firm to the bite.

✛ Remove the risotto from the heat and stir in the remaining ½ tablespoon butter. Taste, and add salt and pepper if needed. Add the Parmesan cheese. Working quickly, spoon the rice into a 2-quart ring mold and press down gently with the wooden spoon to set. Immediately unmold the rice onto a serving platter. Place the quail in the center of the ring and serve.

SERVES 4

✛

The wine I suggest is Amarone from Masi.

Risotto con Calamari, Seppie, e Moscardini

SEAFOOD RISOTTO

4 to 5 fresh squid (about 1½ pounds)
2 small fresh octopus (about 1 pound)
2 fresh seppioline, *or cuttlefish (about*
    1 pound)
3 tablespoons olive oil
1 large garlic clove, crushed
1 small onion, minced
½ cup minced fresh parsley
Salt to taste
Freshly ground black pepper to taste
1 cup dry white wine
2 cups Arborio rice

↦ Thoroughly wash the squid, octopus, and *seppioline* under cold running water. Clean each as follows: Using a sharp knife, cut the tentacles from the sacs where they join. Separate the tentacles into small clumps or, if necessary, cut them into bite-size pieces. Set aside. Remove the long, thin, transparent bones from the sacs. Turn the sacs inside out and remove the stomachs with your fingers. Discard the innards. Slice the sacs into thin rings and set aside with the tentacles.

↦ Place 5 cups water in a covered saucepan over high heat. When the water is hot but not yet simmering, reduce the heat.

↦ Place the olive oil in a large Dutch oven over medium heat. Add the garlic, onion, and parsley and sauté gently until the onion is golden, about 3 minutes.

↦ Add the squid, octopus, and *seppioline* and season with salt and pepper. Add the wine and 1 cup water, reduce the heat to low, and simmer 5 to 8 minutes, or until the liquid has evaporated. Remove the garlic clove.

↦ Add the rice and stir with a wooden spoon for 1 or 2 minutes, until well coated.

↦ Increase the heat to medium-high and add an additional 1 cup water, stirring constantly. When all of the water has been absorbed by the rice, add another 1 cup water and continue stirring. Repeat the process as necessary for approximately 16 minutes, or until the rice is al dente, or firm to the bite.

↦ Remove the risotto from the heat and serve immediately.

SERVES 4

↦

Risotto al Forno

BAKED RISOTTO

4 tablespoons olive oil

1 small onion, finely chopped

2 cups Arborio rice

5 cups Meat Broth (page 27), plus
   additional as needed

Salt to taste

Freshly ground black pepper to taste

Salsa di Pomodori (recipe follows)

⇨ Preheat the oven to 350°F.

⇨ Place the olive oil in a large skillet over medium heat. Add the onion and sauté gently until golden, about 3 minutes.

⇨ Add the rice and stir with a wooden spoon for 1 to 2 minutes, or until the rice is well coated with oil.

⇨ Add 1 cup broth and simmer 2 to 3 minutes, stirring all the while. Pour the rice mixture into a 2-quart baking dish. Add the remaining broth and stir to combine. Bake in the oven for 1 hour, checking occasionally for dryness. If necessary, add more broth to moisten the rice.

⇨ Taste, and season with salt and pepper if needed. Serve very hot, topped with Salsa di Pomodori.

SERVES 4

Salsa di Pomodori

L I G H T   T O M A T O   S A U C E

*2½ pounds fresh plum tomatoes, or 1
  28-ounce can peeled Italian plum
  tomatoes*

½ cup olive oil

1 medium onion, finely chopped

1 cup chopped fresh parsley

Salt to taste

Freshly ground black pepper to taste

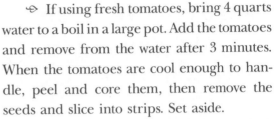 If using fresh tomatoes, bring 4 quarts water to a boil in a large pot. Add the tomatoes and remove from the water after 3 minutes. When the tomatoes are cool enough to handle, peel and core them, then remove the seeds and slice into strips. Set aside.

⊕ Place the olive oil in a large Dutch oven over medium heat. Add the onion and parsley and sauté gently until the onion begins to turn golden, about 3 minutes.

⊕ Add the fresh or canned tomatoes, season with salt and pepper, and turn the heat to medium-high. Cook about 8 minutes, stirring occasionally to prevent sticking. Turn the heat to medium-low and continue simmering until the tomatoes have disintegrated and the oil begins to separate from the sauce, up to 20 minutes.

M A K E S   A B O U T   2½   C U P S

Risotto Nero con le Seppie

BLACK RISOTTO WITH SQUID

Squid is a very tasty and delicate seafood if you buy wisely. Always look for squid that are small, firm-tender, and sweet-smelling.

1½ pounds fresh squid

2 tablespoons olive oil

1 garlic clove

1 small onion, minced

Salt to taste

Freshly ground black pepper to taste

1½ cups dry white wine

2 cups Arborio rice

1 tablespoon unsalted butter

1 cup freshly grated Parmesan cheese

⊷ If your fishmonger won't clean your squid, you can do it yourself: First, wash the squid. Using a sharp knife, cut the tentacles from the sacs where they join. Separate the tentacles into small clumps and set aside. Remove the long, thin transparent bones from the sacs. Turn the sacs inside out and remove the stomachs with your fingers, being careful to keep the ink pouches intact. Discard the stomachs and empty the ink sacs into a small bowl. Slice the sacs into rings and set aside with the tentacles.

⊷ Place 4 to 5 cups water in a covered medium saucepan over high heat. When the water is hot but not yet simmering, reduce the heat to low.

⊷ Place the olive oil in a large Dutch oven over medium heat. Add the garlic and onion and sauté gently until golden, about 3 minutes. Remove the garlic and discard.

⊷ Add the squid, season with salt and pepper, and continue sautéing. After 2 minutes or so, add the wine, reduce the heat to low, and simmer gently about 22 minutes, or until the squid is beginning to become tender.

↭ Add the rice and stir with a wooden spoon for 1 or 2 minutes, or until the rice is well coated with oil. Increase the heat to medium-high and add 1 cup hot water, stirring constantly. When the rice has absorbed most of the liquid, add another 1 cup water and the reserved ink, and continue stirring. Continue adding water and stirring as necessary for approximately 18 minutes, or until the rice is al dente, or firm to the bite.

↭ Remove the risotto from the heat and stir in the butter and Parmesan cheese. Serve immediately.

SERVES 4

↭

A chilled Pinot Grigio goes best with the flavors of this risotto. My favorite producers are Brigl, Banfi, and Boscaini.

Risotto con Salsiccia

RISOTTO WITH SWEET
ITALIAN SAUSAGE

1 quart Meat Broth (page 27)

10 ounces salsiccia *(sweet Italian sausage)*

2 tablespoons olive oil

2 tablespoons unsalted butter

1 small onion, minced

2 cups Arborio rice

Salt to taste

Freshly ground black pepper to taste

↝ Place the broth in a covered medium saucepan over high heat. When the broth is hot but not yet simmering, reduce the heat to low.

↝ Cut the *salsiccia* into 1-inch pieces.

↝ Place the olive oil and butter in a large Dutch oven over medium heat. Add the onion and the sausage and sauté gently until the sausage loses its pink color and the onion is golden.

↝ Add the rice and stir with a wooden spoon for 1 to 2 minutes, or until the rice is well coated with oil.

↝ Increase the heat to medium-high and add 1 cup of the hot broth, stirring constantly. When the rice has absorbed most of the liquid, add another 1 cup broth and continue stirring. Repeat the process as necessary for approximately 16 minutes, or until the rice is al dente, or firm to the bite. Taste and season with salt and pepper if needed.

↝ Remove the risotto from the heat and serve immediately.

SERVES 4
↝

A red wine such as Barbera is delicious with this risotto.

Risotto al Salto

RISOTTO THE NEXT DAY

This excellent dish is made from leftover risotto, and I like it so much that I often make extra risotto with the idea of serving Risotto al Salto the next day. Risotto alla Milanese is really special when prepared this way, but any type of risotto will work well.

✧ Pour a small amount of olive oil in a nonstick skillet or omelet pan. Tilt the pan to lightly coat the entire surface with oil. Press a thin, even layer of leftover risotto into the bottom of the pan and set it over low heat. Let the risotto cook slowly until a golden crust forms in the bottom of the pan. Using a knife or spatula, carefully loosen the risotto from the pan and flip it over like a pancake. Continue cooking until this side, too, is golden and crusty. Loosen the risotto from the pan and carefully slide it onto a serving plate. Cut into wedges and serve immediately.

Risi in Bianco

Rice in Dark Butter

Rice in Butter and Sage

Rice with Garlic

Rice with Egg Yolks

Rice with Parsley

Basil Rice

Rice with Olives

Rice with Peas

Rice with Peas and Red Pepper

Rice with Pistachios and Red Pepper

Rice with Tomato Sauce

Rice with Spinach

Rice with Lentils

Rice in Cheese Sauce

Rice in Gorgonzola Sauce

Rice with Mozzarella

Rice with Shrimp

Rice Mold with Fontina and Gruyère

Rice with Veal Kidneys

Rice-Filled Peppers

Rice-Filled Tomatoes

Rice-Filled Zucchini in Tomato Sauce

Rice with Sweet Sausage

Rice Cake

*R*isi in bianco *are like* risotti *without the fuss. These dishes, built upon the simplicity of plain white Arborio rice, although little discussed in this country, are also an excellent alternative to pasta and represent Italian cooking at its simple, hearty best. Many of my* risi in bianco *recipes are ideal for vegetarians or health-conscious eaters, since they use little fat and feature fresh vegetables. Although these dishes are most often served as* primi piatti, *you may find that with a special salad or soup they can become an elegant, satisfying light meal.*

Riso al Burro Nero

RICE IN DARK BUTTER

2 cups Arborio rice

2 tablespoons unsalted butter

Freshly ground black pepper to taste

2 tablespoons freshly grated Parmesan
    cheese

Salt to taste

⊹ Bring 4 quarts lightly salted water to a boil in a large saucepan. Add the rice and cook, checking for doneness after approximately 18 minutes. Rice should be al dente, or firm to the bite. When the rice is done, remove from the heat and pour into a colander to drain thoroughly.

⊹ Meanwhile, place the butter in a large Dutch oven or deep, heavy skillet over medium heat. Stir the melted butter around with a wooden spoon until it is golden brown in color. (The butter should be more brown than golden; be careful not to let it burn.)

⊹ Pour the rice into the butter and stir vigorously until well coated with the butter, about 2 minutes. Sprinkle on the pepper and Parmesan cheese. Season with salt if necessary and serve immediately.

SERVES 4

⊹

Ceretto, Giacosa, and Pio Cesare are my favorite producers of Barolo, my suggestion for a wine to accompany this dish.

Riso in Bianco al Burro e Salvia

RICE IN BUTTER AND SAGE

This is a very delicate dish, wonderful in any season.

2 cups Arborio rice
2 tablespoons unsalted butter
10 fresh sage leaves
Freshly ground black pepper to taste
½ cup freshly grated Parmesan cheese

↪ Bring 4 quarts lightly salted water to a boil in a large saucepan. Add the rice and cook, checking for doneness after approximately 16 minutes. Rice should be al dente, or firm to the bite; do not overcook. When the rice is done, remove from the heat and pour into a colander to drain completely.

↪ Working quickly, place the butter in a heavy skillet over medium heat. When the butter is foamy, add the sage and stir with a wooden spoon until the butter is golden brown.

↪ Place the drained rice in a serving dish and pour the butter and sage leaves over the top. Season lightly with pepper and serve immediately. Pass the Parmesan cheese at the table.

SERVES 4
↪

Soave, especially that produced by Pieropan, Anselmi, and Masi, is perfect with this dish.

Riso in Bianco all'Aglio

R I C E   W I T H   G A R L I C

8 cups Meat Broth (page 27)

3 tablespoons unsalted butter

3 garlic cloves, minced

2 cups Arborio rice

Salt to taste

Freshly ground black pepper to taste

⭃ Preheat the oven to 350°F.

⭃ Place the broth in a covered medium saucepan over high heat. When the broth begins to boil, reduce the heat to low.

⭃ Meanwhile, place 2 tablespoons butter in a 3-quart flameproof baking dish and set it on the stove over medium heat. When the butter is foamy, add the garlic and sauté until golden.

⭃ Add the rice to the butter mixture and let stand for 1 or 2 minutes. Then pour in the hot broth and bring to a boil.

⭃ Remove the baking dish from the heat and season with salt and pepper. Add the remaining 1 tablespoon butter, cover the dish, and bake for 12 minutes, or until the rice is lightly colored.

⭃ Remove the rice from the oven and serve immediately.

S E R V E S   4

⭃

A robust red wine such as Barbera would be a good choice with this strongly flavored dish.

Riso alle Uova

RICE WITH EGG YOLKS

2 cups Arborio rice

2 jumbo egg yolks

1½ tablespoons unsalted butter

Salt to taste

Freshly ground pepper to taste

½ cup freshly grated Parmesan cheese

↬ Bring 4 quarts lightly salted water to a boil in a large saucepan. Add the rice and cook, checking for doneness after 16 minutes. Rice should be al dente, or firm to the bite; do not overcook. When the rice is cooked, remove from the heat and pour into a colander to drain thoroughly.

↬ Meanwhile, place a 2-quart baking dish in a 350°F. oven to warm. Remove the warmed dish from the oven and pour the rice into it. Pour the egg yolks over the rice and stir vigorously until well mixed, about 1 minute.

↬ Stir in the butter and season with salt and pepper, if necessary. Add the Parmesan cheese and serve immediately.

SERVES 4

↬

Chianti would be a good wine choice with this simple dish.

Riso Caldo al Prezzemolo

RICE WITH PARSLEY

2 cups Arborio rice

1 tablespoon unsalted butter

1½ tablespoons olive oil

½ cup minced fresh parsley

1 large garlic clove

1 cup freshly grated Parmesan cheese

⊷ Bring 4 quarts lightly salted water to a boil in a large saucepan. Add the rice and cook, checking for doneness after approximately 16 minutes. Rice should be al dente, or firm to the bite; do not overcook. When the rice is done, remove from the heat and pour into a colander to drain thoroughly.

⊷ Meanwhile, place the butter and olive oil in a large skillet over medium heat. When the butter begins to foam, add the parsley and the garlic, and sauté gently until the garlic begins to turn golden, about 2 minutes. Remove the garlic and set the sauce aside.

⊷ Place the hot rice in a large serving bowl. Stir in the sauce and the Parmesan cheese and serve immediately.

SERVES 4

⊷

The fresh taste of parsley calls for a light dry white wine such as Orvieto Classico. I suggest the producers Barbi, Antinori, Bigi, and Melini.

Riso al Basilico in Forma

BASIL RICE

This recipe requires the strong flavor that only Pecorino Romano can provide.

2 cups Arborio rice

6 fresh basil leaves, minced

4 tablespoons freshly grated Pecorino Romano cheese

1½ tablespoons olive oil

Salt to taste

2 medium tomatoes, cut into thin wedges, for garnish

Fresh parsley sprigs, for garnish

⁓ Bring 4 quarts lightly salted water to a boil in a large saucepan. Add the rice and cook, checking for doneness after approximately 18 minutes. Rice should be al dente, or firm to the bite; do not overcook. When the rice is done, remove from the heat, pour into a colander, and toss gently to remove excess water.

⁓ Place the hot rice in a large mixing bowl and add the basil and cheese. Stir gently to combine, then add the olive oil and toss thoroughly. Season with salt.

⁓ Spoon the hot rice mixture into a 2-quart mold and press gently to set. Immediately unmold the rice onto a large serving platter. Garnish with tomato wedges and parsley sprigs.

SERVES 4

⁓

This delicate dish needs a dry, chilled white wine such as Soave; try Pieropan, Anselmi, or Masi.

Riso con Olive

RICE WITH OLIVES

2 large red bell peppers

1 cup dry white wine

1 large pinch saffron

1 tablespoon tomato paste

4 tablespoons olive oil

1 tablespoon unsalted butter

1 medium onion, minced

1 small whole fresh chili pepper

2 cups Arborio rice

2 hot Italian sausages (about
     9 ounces)

20 pitted black olives, quartered

Freshly ground black pepper to taste

2 quarts hot Meat Broth (page 27)

↦ Preheat the oven to 350°F.

↦ Wash the bell peppers, then halve them and remove the seeds and any white pith. Cut the peppers into julienne and arrange them in a single layer on a large baking sheet. Place the peppers in the oven and roast 10 minutes, or until the peppers are wilted.

↦ Remove the peppers from the oven and set aside. Place the wine in a small non-metallic bowl, add the saffron and tomato paste, and set aside.

↦ Place the olive oil and the butter in a large Dutch oven over medium-low heat. When the butter is foamy, add the onion and the chili pepper and sauté gently until the onion is wilted but not browned, about 2 minutes.

↦ Add the rice and stir to coat with the oil. Let stand 2 to 3 minutes, then add the sausage, olives, and wine mixture. Increase the heat to medium and simmer approximately 2 minutes, or until the wine has evaporated. Season to taste with black pepper and add the broth. Cover the Dutch oven, reduce the heat to low, and let cook 12 minutes, or until the rice is done—al dente, or firm to the bite.

↦ When the rice is done, remove from the heat and spoon onto a large platter. Scatter the roasted red peppers over the top and serve immediately.

SERVES 4
↦

Serve with Orvieto wine.

Riso in Bianco con Piselli

RICE WITH PEAS

I don't know anyone—child or adult—who doesn't like the combination of rice and peas.

2 cups Arborio rice

2 tablespoons olive oil

4 tablespoons unsalted butter

1 small onion, minced

2½ cups shelled fresh peas, or 2
    16-ounce cans early peas,
    drained, or 1 10-ounce package
    frozen early peas, thawed

1 cup Meat Broth (page 27)

Salt to taste

Freshly ground black pepper to taste

  Bring 4 quarts lightly salted water to a boil in a large saucepan. Add the rice and cook, checking for doneness after approximately 18 minutes. Rice should be al dente, or firm to the bite; do not overcook. When the rice is done, remove from the heat and pour into a colander to drain thoroughly.

  Meanwhile, place the olive oil and half the butter in a large skillet over low heat. When the butter is foamy, add the onion and sauté gently until golden brown, about 2 minutes. Add the peas and stir to coat with the oil. Add the broth, increase the heat to medium, and simmer about 4 minutes, or until the peas are tender. Season with salt and pepper.

  Place the hot rice in a serving dish and stir in the remaining butter. Add the peas, combine thoroughly, and serve immediately. Or spoon the buttered rice into a 2-quart ring mold and press in gently to set. Unmold the rice onto a serving platter and spoon the peas into the center of the ring before serving.

SERVES 4

Red wine can be served with this delightful dish; Rosso di Montalcino would be especially good (look for those produced by Banfi, Col d'Orcia, and Biondi-Santi).

Riso con Piselli e Peperone Rosso

RICE WITH PEAS AND RED PEPPER

2 cups Arborio rice

1 medium red bell pepper

3 tablespoons olive oil

1 10-ounce package frozen early peas, thawed

1 small onion, minced

Salt to taste

Freshly ground pepper to taste

↫ Bring 4 quarts lightly salted water to a boil in a large pan. Add the rice and cook, checking for doneness after approximately 18 minutes. Rice should be al dente, or firm to the bite; do not overcook. When the rice is cooked, remove from the heat and pour into a colander to drain thoroughly.

↫ Meanwhile, wash the bell pepper and halve it. Remove the seeds and any white pith, then cut into julienne and set aside.

↫ Place the olive oil in a large skillet over medium heat. Add the onion and sauté gently until golden, about 2 minutes. Add the bell pepper strips and the peas and cook, stirring, 1 minute longer.

↫ Place the hot rice in a serving bowl and stir in the vegetable mixture. Season with salt and pepper and serve immediately.

SERVES 4

↫

The red pepper gives a strong flavor to this dish. My suggestion is a light red wine like Dolcetto d'Alba.

Riso Tricolore

RICE WITH PISTACHIOS
AND RED PEPPER

2 cups Arborio rice

1 medium red bell pepper

3 tablespoons unsalted butter

2 tablespoons coarsely chopped
unsalted pistachios

1 cup finely chopped fresh parsley

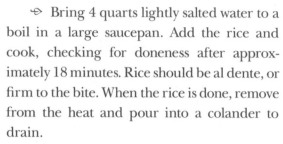

Bring 4 quarts lightly salted water to a boil in a large saucepan. Add the rice and cook, checking for doneness after approximately 18 minutes. Rice should be al dente, or firm to the bite. When the rice is done, remove from the heat and pour into a colander to drain.

Meanwhile, wash the bell pepper and halve it. Remove the seeds and any white pith, then cut into julienne and set aside.

Place the hot rice in a serving bowl, add the butter, and stir gently to mix. Stir in the bell pepper, pistachios, and parsley and serve immediately.

SERVES 4

A Grignolino from the Piedmont would go well with this dish.

Riso in Bianco con Salsa di Pomodori

RICE WITH TOMATO SAUCE

2 tablespoons olive oil

1 medium onion, minced

1 small carrot, finely chopped

*1 28-ounce can peeled Italian
    plum tomatoes, drained and
    coarsely chopped*

Salt to taste

Freshly ground black pepper to taste

2 cups Arborio rice

❧ Place the olive oil in a large skillet over medium heat. Add the onion and the carrot and sauté gently for 2 minutes, or until the onion is golden. Add the tomatoes, season lightly with salt and pepper, and simmer until the tomatoes have disintegrated and oil rises to the surface of the sauce, about 20 minutes. Set the sauce aside.

❧ Bring 4 quarts lightly salted water to a boil in a large saucepan. Add the rice and cook, checking for doneness after approximately 18 minutes. Rice should be al dente, or firm to the bite; do not overcook. When the rice is done, remove from the heat and pour into a colander to drain thoroughly.

❧ Reheat the sauce over medium heat while the rice drains. Place the rice on individual serving plates and spoon the hot sauce over the top.

SERVES 4
❧

A light white wine is most appropriate for this dish; you might like to try a Pinot Grigio, either Bigi or Banfi.

Riso con Spinaci

RICE WITH SPINACH

2 cups Arborio rice

1 pound fresh spinach, washed and
  cleaned, or 2 10-ounce packages
  frozen spinach, thawed

2 tablespoons olive oil

2½ tablespoons unsalted butter

1 large garlic clove

Salt to taste

Freshly ground black pepper to taste

3 tablespoons freshly grated Parmesan
  cheese

↬ Bring 4 quarts lightly salted water to a boil in a large saucepan. Add the rice and cook, checking for doneness after approximately 18 minutes. Rice should be al dente, or firm to the bite; do not overcook. When the rice is done, remove from the heat and pour into a colander to drain thoroughly.

↬ Meanwhile, if using fresh spinach, briefly dunk the leaves in boiling water to soften them, then drain and set aside.

↬ Place the olive oil and 1½ tablespoons butter in a large skillet over low heat. When the butter is foamy, add the garlic and the spinach and sauté gently until the spinach is tender, about 4 minutes. Remove the garlic clove and season the spinach with salt and pepper.

↬ Place the hot rice in a serving bowl and stir in the remaining butter and the sautéed spinach. Sprinkle the Parmesan cheese over the top and serve immediately.

SERVES 4

↬

Riso in Bianco con Lenticchie

RICE WITH LENTILS

As lentils are said to bring good luck, this dish is traditionally served for New Year's Eve.

2 cups (12 ounces) dried lentils
4 tablespoons olive oil, plus additional
for dressing
1 small onion, minced
Salt to taste
Freshly ground black pepper to taste
2 cups Arborio rice

⊕ Wash and pick over the lentils, then cover with warm water and let stand 2 hours. Drain the lentils and set aside.

⊕ Place the olive oil in a skillet or Dutch oven large enough to comfortably hold the lentils. Warm the oil over medium heat, add the onion, and sauté gently for 1½ minutes, or until the onion is soft but not browned. Add the lentils and 3 cups water and season with salt and pepper. Increase the heat to medium and simmer 15 minutes or so, adding more water if necessary, until the lentils are tender.

⊕ Meanwhile, bring 4 quarts lightly salted water to a boil in a large saucepan. Add the rice and cook, checking for doneness after approximately 16 minutes. Rice should be al dente, or firm to the bite; do not overcook. When the rice is done, remove from the heat and pour into a colander to drain thoroughly.

⊕ Heap the rice and the lentils in 2 mounds on a platter and drizzle olive oil over the rice. Serve immediately.

SERVES 4
⊕

This dish is especially good in cold weather and should be served with Chianti da pasto.

Riso alla Crema di Formaggio

RICE IN CHEESE SAUCE

2 cups Arborio rice

1 cup (about 8 ounces) fontina cheese, cut into thin slices

2 tablespoons unsalted butter

¼ cup heavy cream

Salt to taste

Freshly ground black pepper to taste

1 cup freshly grated Parmesan cheese

⥤ Bring 4 quarts lightly salted water to a boil in a large saucepan. Add the rice and cook, checking for doneness after approximately 10 minutes. Rice should be al dente, or firm to the bite. When the rice is done, remove from the heat and pour into a colander to drain thoroughly.

⥤ Preheat the oven to 350°F. Butter a 2-quart baking dish.

⥤ Spread half the drained rice in the bottom of the prepared dish. Top the rice with half the fontina cheese, dot with butter, and drizzle half the cream over the top. Season lightly with salt and pepper. Repeat with the remaining rice, and sprinkle the Parmesan cheese over the top.

⥤ Place the baking dish in the oven and bake 15 to 20 minutes, or until a golden crust has formed. Remove from the oven and serve immediately.

SERVES 4

⥤

A Chianti Classico Riserva from Ruffino, Banfi, or Nozzole will make this simple dish a treat.

Riso in Bianco con Salsa di Gorgonzola

RICE IN GORGONZOLA
SAUCE

4 tablespoons (½ stick) unsalted butter

6 ounces (⅔ cup) Gorgonzola cheese,
    crumbled

½ cup half-and-half

½ cup dry white wine

Salt to taste

Freshly ground black pepper to taste

2 cups Arborio rice

4 fresh basil leaves, for garnish

↬ Place the butter in a medium saucepan over low heat. When the butter has melted, add the Gorgonzola, then increase the heat to medium and continue cooking 2 to 3 minutes. When the cheese is melted, add the half-and-half and the wine. Stir with a wooden spoon to combine and continue cooking until the sauce is thickened, about 1½ minutes. Remove from the heat, season with salt and pepper, and set aside.

↬ Bring 4 quarts lightly salted water to a boil in a large saucepan. Add the rice and cook, checking for doneness after approximately 16 minutes. Rice should be al dente, or firm to the bite. When the rice is done, remove from the heat and pour into a colander to drain thoroughly.

↬ Place the cheese sauce over medium-low heat and warm carefully. Taste and adjust seasonings if necessary.

↬ Spoon the hot rice onto a large serving platter and drizzle the sauce over the top. Garnish with the basil leaves and serve immediately.

SERVES 4

↬

Cantina Produttori Nebbiolo di Carema and Caves Cooperatives de Donnaz are two of my favorite producers of Carema, my first choice for wine with this dish.

Riso Caldo con Mozzarella

RICE WITH MOZZARELLA

2 cups Arborio rice

½ pound fresh mozzarella cheese, cut into bite-size cubes

5 ounces boiled ham, cut into bite-size cubes (about ½ cup)

2 large egg yolks, lightly beaten

2 tablespoons freshly grated Parmesan cheese

Salt to taste

↞ Bring 4 quarts lightly salted water to a boil in a large saucepan. Add the rice and cook, checking for doneness after approximately 18 minutes. Rice should be al dente, or firm to the bite; do not overcook. When the rice is done, remove from the heat and pour into a colander to drain thoroughly.

↞ Place the mozzarella and ham in a large mixing bowl. Add the hot rice, egg yolks, Parmesan cheese, and the salt. Toss gently to combine. Serve immediately.

SERVES 4

↞

122

Riso in Bianco Agli Scampi

RICE WITH SHRIMP

SHRIMP SAUCE

½ tablespoon unsalted butter

1½ tablespoons olive oil

1 medium onion, minced

1 celery stalk, minced

1 large carrot, minced

½ cup brandy

1 cup dry white wine

12 fresh medium shrimp (about 1
    pound), shelled and deveined,
    with tails left on

Salt to taste

6 cups Meat Broth (page 27)

2 cups Arborio rice

½ tablespoon unsalted butter

↬ Prepare the shrimp sauce. Place the butter and olive oil for the sauce in a large skillet over medium heat. When the butter is foamy, add the onion, celery, and carrot and sauté gently until the onion begins to turn golden, about 2 minutes. Add the brandy, wine, and shrimp; season with salt and simmer gently 15 minutes, or until the shrimp are done and the sauce is somewhat thickened. Remove from the heat and set aside.

↬ Bring the broth to a boil in a covered saucepan. Add the rice, reduce the heat to low, and simmer until the rice is done, about 16 minutes. Rice should be al dente, or firm to the bite; do not overcook.

↬ Drain the rice, toss with the butter, and spread it over a large serving platter. Gently reheat the shrimp sauce and spoon it over the rice. Serve immediately.

SERVES 4

↬

Pinot Bianco is an excellent wine choice for this dish.

Timballo di Riso con Fontina e Gruviera

RICE MOLD WITH
FONTINA AND GRUYERE

2 cups Arborio rice

3 tablespoons unsalted butter

4 tablespoons freshly grated Parmesan cheese

6 ounces fontina cheese, thinly sliced (about ⅔ cup)

6 ounces Gruyère or Swiss cheese, thinly sliced (about ⅔ cup)

6 ounces boiled ham, cut into bite-size pieces (about ⅔ cup)

◈ Bring 4 quarts lightly salted water to a boil in a large saucepan. Add the rice and cook, checking for doneness after approximately 18 minutes. Rice should be al dente, or firm to the bite; do not overcook. When the rice is done, remove from the heat and pour into a colander to drain thoroughly.

◈ Place the hot rice in a large mixing bowl. Add 2½ tablespoons of the butter and the Parmesan cheese and toss to combine.

◈ Preheat the oven to 350°F. Grease a 2-quart baking dish or ring mold with the remaining ½ tablespoon butter.

◈ Spoon one-third of the rice into the prepared baking dish or mold and spread it evenly over the bottom. Top with one-third each of the fontina, Gruyère, and the ham. Repeat until all the ingredients have been incorporated.

◈ Bake for 5 minutes, or until the cheese is bubbly and the rice is lightly browned. If using a mold, submerge to the rim in hot water for a minute or two, then invert the mold onto a large platter. Serve immediately.

SERVES 4

◈

Gruyère is a pungent cheese, so I would recommend serving a full-bodied red wine like a Barbera.

Riso in Bianco con Rognoncini di Vitello

R I C E   W I T H   V E A L   K I D N E Y S

2 small veal kidneys (about 12 ounces)
1 cup red wine vinegar, or as needed
2 cups Arborio rice
½ tablespoon unsalted butter
3 tablespoons olive oil
1 cup chopped fresh parsley
½ cup dry red or white wine

✤ Wash the veal kidneys under cold running water for a few minutes. With a sharp knife, remove any fat or white membrane from the kidneys. Slice the kidneys very thin and place in a shallow nonmetallic bowl. Add red wine vinegar to cover, then refrigerate 2 hours, occasionally turning the kidney slices in the marinade.

✤ When ready to eat, bring 4 quarts lightly salted water to a boil in a large pan. Add the rice and cook, checking for doneness after approximately 16 minutes. Rice should be al dente, or firm to the bite; do not overcook. When the rice is done, remove from the heat and pour into a colander to drain thoroughly.

✤ While the rice is cooking, place the butter and 1 tablespoon olive oil in a large skillet over medium heat. Remove the kidney slices from the refrigerator and drain. When the butter is foamy, add the sliced kidneys and sauté over high heat until they begin to lose their pink color, about 3 minutes. Add the parsley and the wine and simmer about 1½ minutes, or until the kidneys are cooked through.

✤ Place the hot rice in a large mixing bowl and toss with the remaining 2 tablespoons olive oil. Spoon the rice into a 2-quart ring mold, pressing down gently to set. Invert the mold onto a large platter and spoon the kidneys and their sauce into the center of the ring. Serve immediately.

S E R V E S   4
✤

This is a wonderful dish, to be served with a special wine. You might try a chilled Pinot Grigio or, my choice, Brunello di Montalcino.

Peperoni Ripieni di Riso

RICE-FILLED PEPPERS

2 cups Arborio rice

3 large red bell peppers

3 large yellow bell peppers

Unsalted butter

6 tablespoons olive oil

7 pitted green olives, minced

1 tablespoon capers, minced

Salt to taste

Freshly ground black pepper to taste

1 teaspoon fresh oregano leaves

1 cup chopped fresh parsley

7 salted anchovies

⊸ Bring 4 quarts lightly salted water to a boil in a large saucepan. Add the rice and cook, checking for doneness after approximately 18 minutes. Rice should be al dente, or firm to the bite. When the rice is done, pour into a colander to drain thoroughly.

⊸ Meanwhile, wash the peppers and cut them in half crosswise. Remove the stems, seeds, and any white pith and set aside.

⊸ Preheat the oven to 350°F. Butter a shallow baking dish large enough to hold the 6 pepper halves.

⊸ Wash the anchovies in cold water and chop them into small pieces.

⊸ Place the rice in a large mixing bowl and add the olive oil, olives, anchovies, and capers. Stir gently to combine. Season with salt and pepper and stir in the oregano and parsley.

⊸ Spoon the rice mixture into the pepper halves, mounding the rice gently over the top. Arrange the stuffed peppers in the dish.

⊸ Bake for 30 minutes, or until the peppers are tender. Remove from the oven and serve immediately. Or, if you prefer, allow the peppers to cool, then refrigerate them overnight. Served chilled, they make a delicious luncheon dish on a hot day.

SERVES 4

⊸

My wine choice would be a cold, dry white wine—Bianco di Chianti.

Pomodori Freddi Ripieni di Riso

RICE-FILLED TOMATOES

1½ cups Arborio rice

4 firm medium tomatoes

4 Greek olives, minced

2 medium yellow bell peppers, seeded and finely diced

2 medium red bell peppers, seeded and finely diced

1 celery stalk, minced

3 tablespoons chopped fresh parsley

4 fresh basil leaves, chopped

Juice of 2 lemons

3 tablespoons olive oil

Salt to taste

Freshly ground black pepper to taste

⤜ Bring 4 quarts lightly salted water to a boil in a large saucepan. Add the rice and cook, checking for doneness after approximately 16 minutes. Rice should be al dente, or firm to the bite; do not overcook. When the rice is done, remove from the heat and pour into a colander to drain thoroughly.

⤜ Meanwhile, wash the tomatoes and pat dry. With a sharp knife, slice off the top fifth of each tomato, including the stem, and set aside. Using a spoon, scoop out the soft inner pulp of the tomatoes, leaving a ¼-inch or slightly thicker shell intact. Set the tomato shells aside and reserve. Press the tomato pulp through a sieve to remove the seeds, then place the pulp in a large mixing bowl.

⤜ Add the olives, bell peppers, celery, parsley, basil, and lemon juice to the tomato pulp. Add the rice and toss gently to combine. Drizzle the olive oil over the top, season with salt and pepper, and toss again.

⤜ Spoon the rice mixture into the tomato shells, pressing gently to smooth the rice. Place the tomatoes in a shallow dish and replace the reserved tomato tops. Cover with plastic wrap and chill in the refrigerator 6 hours before serving.

SERVES 4

⤜

Complement this dish with a chilled white wine such as Orvieto Classico from Barbi, Antinori, or Barberani.

Zucchine Ripiene di Riso in Salsa di Pomodori al Forno

RICE-FILLED ZUCCHINI
IN TOMATO SAUCE

TOMATO SAUCE

1½ tablespoons unsalted butter

3 tablespoons olive oil

1 medium onion, minced

1 16-ounce can peeled Italian plum
tomatoes

4 fresh basil leaves

Salt to taste

4 large zucchini

1½ cups Arborio rice

3 tablespoons unsalted butter, plus
additional

✧ Prepare the tomato sauce. Place the butter and olive oil in a large skillet over medium heat. When the butter is foamy, add the onion and sauté gently until golden, about 1½ minutes. Add the tomatoes, lower the heat, and simmer gently for 25 minutes. Add the basil, stir, and continue simmering an additional 20 minutes, or until the oil begins to separate from the sauce. Taste, and add salt if necessary. Remove from the heat and set aside.

✧ Wash and trim the zucchini.

✧ Bring 4 quarts lightly salted water to a rapid boil in a large saucepan. Plunge the zucchini into the boiling water and blanch 2 minutes. Remove the zucchini and place in a colander to cool.

✧ Meanwhile, bring another 4 quarts lightly salted water to a boil in a large saucepan. Add the rice and cook, checking for doneness after approximately 16 minutes. Rice should be al dente, or firm to the bite; do not overcook. When the rice is done, remove from the heat and pour into a colander to drain thoroughly.

✧ Preheat the oven to 350°F. Butter a shallow baking dish large enough to hold 8 zucchini halves in a single layer.

✧ Place the hot rice in a large mixing bowl and toss with the butter. Slice the cooled zucchini in half horizontally. Using a spoon, scoop out the seeds and some of the flesh from each zucchini half, leaving a sturdy shell.

Spoon the rice into each hollowed-out zucchini, pressing down gently to set. Place the filled zucchini in the prepared baking dish and pour the tomato sauce over evenly.

    ↬ Bake for 15 to 20 minutes, or until the rice is lightly browned. Serve immediately or, if you prefer, allow to cool, then chill in the refrigerator before serving.

S E R V E S   4

↬

Because this dish has strong flavors and can be served cold, a red wine would be a nice accompaniment.

Riso alla Salsiccia

RICE WITH SWEET SAUSAGE

1½ tablespoons unsalted butter

2 sweet Italian sausages (about 9
      ounces), cut into bite-size pieces

2 cups Arborio rice

1 cup freshly grated Parmesan cheese

    ↬ Place the butter in a large skillet over medium heat. When the butter is foamy, add the sausages and sauté gently until done, about 15 minutes, taking care not to let the butter burn.

    ↬ Meanwhile, bring 4 quarts lightly salted water to a boil in a large saucepan. Add the rice and cook, checking for doneness after approximately 18 minutes. Rice should be al dente, or firm to the bite; do not overcook. When the rice is done, remove from the heat and pour into a colander to drain thoroughly.

    ↬ Place the rice in a large serving bowl. Add the sausages and the Parmesan cheese and toss gently. Serve immediately.

S E R V E S   4

Tortino di Riso

RICE CAKE

This makes a delightful dinner on a cold winter night.

2 cups milk

Salt to taste

1½ cups Arborio rice

2 tablespoons unsalted butter

5 tablespoons freshly grated Parmesan cheese

4 large eggs, separated

Freshly ground black pepper to taste

⊷ Place the milk and salt in a large lidded saucepan and bring to a boil over high heat. Add the rice, cover, and reduce the heat to low. Let cook 15 minutes, stirring occasionally, until the liquid has been absorbed and the rice is al dente, or firm to the bite.

⊷ Remove the rice from the heat and stir in 1 tablespoon of the butter, the Parmesan cheese, and the egg yolks. Stir to combine thoroughly and season to taste with pepper. Set aside.

⊷ Preheat the oven to 350°F. Coat the inside of a 1½-quart baking dish with the remaining 1 tablespoon butter.

⊷ Beat the egg whites thoroughly with a whisk or electric mixer until stiff but not dry. Fold the beaten whites into the rice and spoon the mixture into the prepared dish.

⊷ Place the dish in the oven and bake 30 minutes, or until the top of the rice cake is golden. Remove from the oven and loosen the edges of the cake with a knife. Invert the rice cake onto a platter and serve immediately.

SERVES 4

⊷

Dolci

DESSERTS

Banana Rice Pudding
Rice Pudding with Fruit
Rice with Cantaloupe
Rice-Filled Peaches
Rice with Cream and Ricotta
Rice Fritters
Rice Cake with Grand Marnier

*A*lthough Italian regional cuisine offers some delicious cakes and dolci al cucchiaio *(sweets eaten with a spoon), it does not boast a tremendous variety of desserts. Italy is a country blessed with sunshine and, thus, what there is is a tremendous variety of sweet, sun-ripened fruits. The favorite Italian way to end a meal is with a delectable assortment of oranges, plums, grapes, peaches, apricots, or figs. In fact, even when a prepared dessert is served, it is most often accompanied by a selection of fresh fruits.*

What you'll find in this chapter are a few of my favorite Italian desserts, all based on rice.

Riso Bianco al Forno con Banana

BANANA RICE PUDDING

2½ cups milk

2 cups Arborio rice

2 large egg whites

2 large ripe bananas, thoroughly
*   mashed*

1 large egg yolk, lightly beaten

1½ tablespoons unsalted butter, plus
*   additional*

↬ Preheat the oven to 350°F. Butter a 2-quart baking dish.

↬ Place the milk in a medium saucepan over high heat and bring to a boil. Add the rice, cover, reduce the heat to low, and cook about 18 minutes, until the rice is al dente, or firm to the bite. While the rice is cooking, beat the egg whites until stiff but not dry.

↬ Remove the rice from the heat and stir in the bananas. Using a wooden spoon, quickly stir in the egg yolk and the butter until thoroughly incorporated. Continue beating the rice mixture with the wooden spoon and fold in the egg whites.

↬ Pour the mixture into the prepared baking dish. Bake for 10 minutes, or until the top is golden and crusty.

↬ Remove the pudding from the oven and allow to cool slightly. Use a sharp knife to loosen the pudding from the edges of the baking dish, then invert onto a serving dish. Serve immediately.

SERVES 4

Budino di Riso con Frutta

RICE PUDDING WITH FRUIT

2 cups milk

2 cups Arborio rice

3½ tablespoons sugar

1 tablespoon unsalted butter

1 apple, peeled and cut into bite-size
    pieces

1 firm ripe banana, cut into bite-size
    pieces

1 pint strawberries, hulled and cut
    into bite-size pieces

Juice of 2 lemons

↬ Place the milk in a medium saucepan over high heat and bring to a boil. Add the rice, cover, reduce the heat to low, and cook 16 minutes, until the rice is al dente, or firm to the bite.

↬ Preheat the oven to 350°F. Meanwhile, place ½ tablespoon of the sugar in a small saucepan with 3 tablespoons water. Bring to a boil and cook until the sugar water begins to thicken and turn caramel colored. Remove the syrup from the heat and pour into a 2-quart ring mold. Tilt the mold quickly to coat all surfaces before the syrup hardens.

↬ When the rice is done, remove from the heat and stir in the butter and the remaining 3 tablespoons sugar. Spoon the rice into the prepared mold and smooth the top. Set the mold inside a baking pan at least 4 inches deep.

↬ Place the baking pan in the oven and carefully pour in 3 inches boiling water. Bake about 20 minutes, or until golden and crusty.

↬ Remove the pudding from the oven and allow to cool slightly, then chill in the refrigerator at least 30 minutes. Stir together the fruit pieces and the lemon juice. Chill.

↬ When ready to serve, remove the pudding from the refrigerator. Using a sharp knife, loosen the edges of the pudding from the mold, then invert onto a serving platter. Spoon the fruit mixture into the center of the pudding and serve.

SERVES 4

↬

Riso con Melone

RICE WITH CANTALOUPE

2 cups Arborio rice

2 cups milk

2 ripe cantaloupes

5 tablespoons sugar

1 tablespoon ground cinnamon

❧ Bring 4 quarts lightly salted water to a boil in a large saucepan. Add the rice and cook 10 minutes. Remove the rice from the heat and drain in a colander. Rinse the rice with cool water and allow to drain again.

❧ Meanwhile, place the milk in a medium saucepan and bring to a boil over high heat. Add the partly cooked rice, cover, reduce the heat to low, and cook exactly 8 minutes, no longer. Rice should be al dente, or firm to the bite. Remove the rice from the heat and allow to cool.

❧ Cut the cantaloupes in half lengthwise, then scoop out and discard the seeds. Scoop out the cantaloupe flesh and reserve the rinds. Cut the cantaloupe flesh into bite-size pieces. Set aside.

❧ When the rice is cooled completely, add the sugar and cinnamon and stir in. Add the melon and mix thoroughly. Spoon the rice mixture into the reserved cantaloupe shells. Chill in the refrigerator at least 30 minutes before serving.

SERVES 4

❧

Pesche Ripiene di Riso

RICE-FILLED PEACHES

These luscious peaches are good hot or cold.

3½ cups milk

2 cups Arborio rice

2 large egg yolks

2 tablespoons granulated sugar

5 large ripe yellow peaches

1 teaspoon unsalted butter

2 teaspoons confectioners' sugar

❧ Place 2 cups of the milk in a medium saucepan over high heat and bring to a boil. Add the rice, cover, reduce the heat to low, and cook about 15 minutes, until the rice is al dente, or firm to the bite.

❧ Meanwhile, place the remaining 1½ cups milk in another medium saucepan and set over medium heat. In a small bowl, beat together the egg yolks and the granulated sugar. When the milk is hot, stir a small amount into the yolk mixture to warm it, then quickly whisk the yolks into the hot milk. Stir constantly until the custard thickens and coats the back of a spoon, 2 to 3 minutes. Do not allow to boil. Set the custard aside to cool, stirring occasionally to prevent a skin.

❧ Wash the peaches and cut them in half. Remove the pits and scoop out most of the pulp with a spoon, leaving a ¼-inch shell of peach flesh.

❧ Preheat the oven to 350°F. Butter a shallow baking dish large enough to hold the 10 peach halves.

❧ Stir the rice into the cooled custard. Spoon the mixture into the peach halves, mounding the tops. Place the filled peaches in the prepared baking dish and sprinkle the tops with the confectioners' sugar.

❧ Bake in the oven 15 to 20 minutes, or until the rice turns golden and crusty.

❧ Remove the peaches from the oven and serve immediately. Or, if desired, allow the peaches to cool to room temperature, then chill in the refrigerator at least 2 hours.

SERVES 5

❧

This dessert is just right with a glass of port; try Fonseca, Sandeman, or Dow & Taylor.

Riso in Bianco alla Panna e Ricotta

RICE WITH CREAM AND RICOTTA

2 cups Arborio rice

Unsalted butter

1 cup heavy cream

1 large egg

½ pound (1 cup) ricotta cheese

1 cup freshly grated Parmesan cheese

*½ cup raisins, soaked in 3 tablespoons
    rum*

⇔ Bring 4 quarts lightly salted water to a boil in a large saucepan. Add the rice and cook 16 to 18 minutes. Rice should be al dente, or firm to the bite; do not overcook. When the rice is done, remove from the heat, pour into a colander, and rinse with cool water. Set the rice aside to cool completely.

⇔ Butter a 2-quart mold.

⇔ Whip the cream until stiff peaks form.

⇔ In a large mixing bowl, beat the egg briskly with a fork. Stir in the cooled rice, ricotta, Parmesan, and the raisins, with any unabsorbed rum. Mix thoroughly, then stir in the whipped cream. Spoon the rice mixture into the prepared mold and smooth the top. Chill in the refrigerator at least 1 hour before serving.

SERVES 4

⇔

Frittelle di Riso

RICE FRITTERS

These *frittelle* are originally from Pistoia in Tuscany. When I was a child, my mother hired mostly women from Tuscany to work in our house because of their good command of Italian (many were educated in convents) and also because they were usually excellent cooks and even better embroiderers.

4 cups milk

Salt

1½ cups Arborio rice

2 large eggs

1 tablespoon all-purpose flour

Grated rind of 1 orange

Grated rind of 1 lemon

Pinch of salt

Granulated sugar to taste

Oil for frying (enough to just cover the frittelle)

½ cup confectioners' sugar

↬ Place 2 cups of the milk with a pinch of salt in a heavy medium saucepan over high heat. When the milk begins to boil, add the rice and reduce the heat to medium. Meanwhile, place the remaining 2 cups milk in a smaller saucepan and heat until just below the boiling point. When the rice has absorbed the milk, add the hot milk and continue cooking. After 16 to 18 minutes, the rice should be al dente, or firm to the bite.

↬ Remove the rice from the stove and stir in the eggs, flour, and orange and lemon rinds. When well blended, stir in a pinch of salt and granulated sugar to taste.

↬ Heat the oil in a large, heavy frying pan. When hot, drop tablespoons of the rice mixture into the oil and fry 4 to 5 minutes, or until the first side is golden. Turn the fritters and continue frying until the other side is golden.

↬ Remove the fritters from the hot oil with tongs and place on paper towels to drain. Transfer the fritters to a platter in a 250°F. oven until all have been fried and drained.

↬ Sprinkle the hot fritters with the confectioners' sugar and serve immediately.

SERVES 4

↬

Torta di Riso al Grand Marnier

RICE CAKE WITH GRAND MARNIER

This is a delicious treat at any meal, in any season.

6 cups milk

Pinch of salt

1½ cups Arborio rice

Grated rind of 1 lemon

4 tablespoons sugar

3 large eggs

2 tablespoons unsalted butter

1 large egg yolk, lightly beaten

2 tablespoons finely diced candied citron

2 cups (½ pound) slivered almonds, toasted

2½ tablespoons Grand Marnier liqueur

1½ tablespoons bread crumbs

↝ Place the milk and salt in a heavy saucepan over high heat. When the milk boils, add the rice and lemon rind, reduce the heat to low, and cook, covered, for 16 to 18 minutes, or until the rice is al dente, or firm to the bite. Remove from the heat.

↝ Stir the sugar, eggs, and butter into the rice until well blended, then set aside to cool.

↝ When the rice is lukewarm throughout, stir in the egg yolk, candied citron, almonds, and liqueur.

↝ Preheat the oven to 300°F. Butter an 8-inch square baking dish. Sprinkle the bread crumbs over the bottom of the dish and tilt to coat the sides. Pour in the rice mixture and smooth the top.

↝ Place the dish in the oven and bake 40 to 45 minutes, or until a golden crust forms. The cake is done when a toothpick inserted in the center comes out dry.

↝ Remove the cake from the oven and allow to cool. Serve at room temperature.

SERVES 4

↝

Index